Lighten Up

Also by Charles Stuart Platkin

Breaking the Pattern
Breaking the Fat Pattern

Lighten Up

Stay Sane, Eat Great, Lose Weight

By Charles Stuart Platkin

razOr
bill

Lighten Up: Stay Sane, Eat Great, Lose Weight

RAZORBILL

Published by the Penguin Group Penguin Young Readers Group
345 Hudson Street, New York, New York 10014, U.S.A.

Penguin Group (USA) Inc., 375 Hudson Street, New York, New York 10014, U.S.A.
Penguin Group (Canada), 90 Eglinton Avenue, Suite 700, Toronto, Ontario,
    Canada M4P 2Y3 (a division of Pearson Penguin Canada Inc.)
Penguin Books Ltd, 80 Strand, London WC2R 0RL, England
Penguin Ireland, 25 St Stephen's Green, Dublin 2, Ireland
    (a division of Penguin Books Ltd)
Penguin Group (Australia), 250 Camberwell Road, Camberwell,
    Victoria 3124, Australia (a division of Pearson Australia Group Pty Ltd)
Penguin Books India Pvt Ltd, 11 Community Centre,
    Panchsheel Park, New Delhi—110 017, India
Penguin Group (NZ), Cnr Airborne and Rosedale Roads, Albany,
    Auckland 1310, New Zealand (a division of Pearson New Zealand Ltd)
Penguin Books (South Africa) (Pty) Ltd, 24 Sturdee Avenue,
    Rosebank, Johannesburg 2196, South Africa

Penguin Books Ltd, Registered Offices: 80 Strand, London WC2R 0RL, England

10 9 8 7 6 5 4 3 2

Interior design by Alan Barnett, Inc.

Library of Congress Cataloging-in-Publication Data

Platkin, Charles Stuart.
    Lighten up : stay sane, eat great, lose weight / by Charles Stuart Platkin.
        p. cm.
    Includes index.
    ISBN 1-59514-065-4
    1. Weight loss. 2. Physical fitness. 3. Health behavior. I. Title.
RM222.2.P5665 2005
613.2'5—dc22

2005023907

Printed in the United States of America

This book is dedicated to my daughter,
Parker South, a constant inspiration; to my parents,
Linda and Norton, who have always and continue to be
a driving force in my life; and to my wife, a patient,
considerate, and caring friend, Shannon.

Table of Contents

INTRODUCTION What's Keeping You From Having the Body You Want?

- Do you have a slow metabolism?
- Is willpower missing from your genes?
- Have you decided that you're destined to be overweight?
- Or is your school cafeteria destined to serve the same fattening foods until you graduate?
- Have you tried a diet or two (or five) and felt disappointed?
- Have you tried a diet or two that made you disappointed in *yourself?*
- Is it too hard give up McDonald's Big Mac and large fries?
- Or is it too hard to imagine you could ever actually be in shape?

No matter what the reason, *something*—maybe everything— is keeping you from that body you wish you had. And right now you're probably wondering, can this book help? Can *anything?*

I'm here to tell you that at this very moment, you hold the key to getting your wish. You are completely capable of putting that extra weight—whether it's five pounds or fifty— behind you for good, sooner than you think. And this book is going to give you everything you need.

A DIET THAT WORKS

Before you ask if I'm going to promise you a fancy car and a mansion in Hollywood, too, let me explain!

If you've tried dieting, you know that lots of diets help you lose weight: The problem is that you always end up gaining it back. Most diets give you a list of rules designed by someone who doesn't know *you*. Almost all diets make you feel deprived of the things you like—until you give in to temptation and end up thinking, "If only I had enough willpower...."

Well, the fact is that trying to find an extra-amazing stash of willpower is a lot like trying to land a date with Orlando Bloom or Keira Knightley for the senior prom: *It's probably not going to happen.* Not for me, you, or anyone else.

➔ To get the body you want, you don't have to deprive yourself of the foods you love, or go on a quick-fix diet you can't stick to, or dig up a dose of monster-size willpower. All you have to do is change the way you *think* about eating. Once you do that, changing the way you eat will become automatic.

That's where this book comes in. Lightening up is not about willpower, or rules, or sacrifices. It's not about passing trends or empty promises. It's about a diet that's easy enough and satisfying enough to stick with forever because you're making the compromises *you* choose. And it works for real, and for good.

Empower, Not Willpower

Most people try to use willpower to make changes that really require *empowerment*. What do I mean by that? Empowerment means giving *yourself* the power to lose weight, and you can do that by changing your behavior. We're not talking huge, overwhelming changes. Just small ones you can live with. You're about to learn how.

Shhhh!

Here's a secret that all successful dieters share: The one surefire way to lose weight and keep it off is to make the kind of eating choices you don't even have to think about.

Remember learning to ride a bike? Remember how at first it seemed like there was a lot to think about, and then one day it just became unconscious and...automatic? Same thing.

Most diets leave out one crucial ingredient: **you**. *Lighten Up* works because *it's all about you.*

SO HOW DO I KNOW ALL THIS?

Before I figured out the steps I'll give you in this book, I spent way too much time being overweight...and miserable about it. I know only too well that if you've never been thin, it's hard to imagine it's really possible (it is!)—and it's hard to visualize how much better life can be with a thin, healthy body. That's not superficial—it's just a fact.

From my tenth birthday on, I was trying every diet out there, including Dr. Atkins' diet book (yeah, it actually came out that many years ago). Some of the diets seemed foolproof...at first. Lots of them helped me lose the weight...for a while. But the weight always came back, over and over, like the world's most depressing diet yo-yo.

Once I learned to build a diet that was automatic—a diet that fit *me*—I lost the weight and kept it off for good. Getting and keeping a thin, healthy body had such a major impact on my life that I realized I wanted to help other people do the same thing. Since then, I've founded a health company, written lots of articles, and helped tons of people get into top shape. I guess you could call nutrition and fitness my passion.

I don't think of myself as a "diet guru." And I'm not selling a trendy diet. More than anything, I'm a guy who's been there—and found a way to triumph over my weight. I'm someone who figured out there was a simple, real way to get thin and stay there—and I've been told by countless people that I'm good at helping others do the same thing. I *know* I can help *you*.

TEN STEPS: YOUR STYLE

Here's how it works.

I've created ten steps that will help you make the small changes—in your eating, in your thinking, in your day-to-day activities—that will create big changes in your weight.

It starts with the basics. In Step 1, I'll talk about trendy diets—how they work *and* don't work. From there we'll move on to building your real, automatic diet from the ground up.

I'll ask you to fill in all sorts of stuff about yourself, including quizzes and questionnaires, **so have a pen or pencil ready.**

And by the way, feel free to jump around the book. *Lighten Up* is all about your own pace and your own style.

Lighten Up **Will Include...**

- A custom-built plan for losing weight that helps you look at your life and make minor adjustments that last
- Secret weapons against your worst diet downfalls
- Amazing diet mind tricks
- Excuse Busters!
- Diet-trap escape routes
- Surprising ways to get physical...and actually like it

And much more!

You might say, "I don't *want* to have to 'work' out the details of a diet. That sounds too hard! I'd rather follow someone else's diet." My answer to that comes in two parts. First, creating an automatic diet is not hard at all—it's just a matter of reading this book. And second, other people's rules *don't work!* The only person who can make a diet that works for you forever is you!

When you've finished all ten steps, you'll have a diet that fits like a glove and the power to stick to it forever.

You're Ready for This Book If...

- You'd love to lose five pounds.
- You'd love to lose forty pounds.
- You've been overweight since you can remember.
- You've been overweight since last Christmas.
- You're sick of having to squeeze through the aisles in your classrooms.
- You're sick of trying to squeeze into last year's jeans.
- You want a slim, healthy body that will get you positive attention.
- You've been teased for being overweight, and it's uncomfortable.
- You're tired of wanting to lose weight but never really trying.
- You're tired of dieting all the time with disappointing results.
- You're just plain tired of carrying around those extra pounds.

STEP 1 Get Diet-Savvy

DO YOU BELIEVE IN MIRACLES?

Maybe you've heard of them. Maybe you've seen them. Maybe your friends have tried them, and maybe you have.

They're the latest diet sensations. They offer no-brainer ways to lose weight—like simply giving up carbs, or staying away from fat, or only eating frozen meals, or simply drinking a shake twice a day, or just eating the way the French do. They all have sexy spokesmodels gushing over their life-changing properties. They make it look oh so easy. And they make it simple by telling you exactly what to do to get the body you want...by tomorrow!

They're trendy diets, and for many reasons, they seem irresistible. There's always a reason why one is supposed to be easier and work better and faster than all the rest:

- All the burger, but no fries
- All the fries, but no burger
- All the milk shakes, but no solid food

But here's a great reason you'll *want* to resist them. Hopefully it will change the way you look at diets forever. Are you ready?

 Everyone who goes on a trendy diet ends up *gaining* weight... sooner or later.

Join the 2% Club

According to the latest research, about *98%* of the people who diet gain the weight back. ***98%!*** That means only 2% of people who lose weight keep it off. And most of those people use strategies like the ones in this book. Want to join the 2% club? Keep going!

Don't believe me? Keep reading. We haven't even scratched the surface yet.

WHY TRENDY DIETS HAPPEN TO GOOD PEOPLE

First things first. We've got to get one thing straight: *Dieting is big business.*

Diet gurus and diet companies are selling their products to you in any way they can. Listen to Anna Nicole Smith on the radio, watch all the low-carb ads on TV, or walk through any GNC at the mall, and you'll hear about all these companies that have finally developed the plan to beat all plans, the shake to beat all shakes, the diet miracle that will change *everything.*

After all, lots of people are making money off your desire for a thinner body. They'll tell you anything to get you to buy. But what they won't tell you is what I've already mentioned above: These kinds of diets usually help you lose weight— only to *gain* it back.

If you've experienced this firsthand, it may have left you feeling like a huge failure. You may have poured your energy into a diet—and it worked for a little while, but it didn't hold up. Or it never worked at all. Or it made things worse.

Why not refuse to buy into the hype, and get a plan that works—permanently and without depriving you of food?

DIET IS A FOUR-LETTER WORD

One of the biggest problems is that too many people are confused about what a *real* diet really is, or what it can be.

For starters, when you hear the word *diet,* what do you think of? (Check all that apply.)

❏ Giving up the food I like for a better body

❏ Something I'm always screwing up. If I only had enough willpower, I'd lose the weight.

❏ Eating celery sticks while my friends are eating burgers and fries

❏ Skipping meals

❏ Stuffing my face with a bag of potato chips—and feeling guilty about it for the rest of the day

❏ Something that people have to get lucky at. If I pick the right diet, it'll work.

❏ Something I've never tried, or tried only barely

❏ Something that'll never work for me: I've never been thin, and I probably never will be

Now guess what the word *diet* really means....(Circle one.)

a. Cutting calories to lose weight

b. Cutting down on fat to lose weight

c. Focusing on a certain kind of food to lose weight

d. Food and drink regularly consumed

If you chose A, B, or C, get ready to be surprised. The bona fide dictionary definition of *diet* is "food and drink regularly consumed" *(Merriam-Webster Online Dictionary). That's it.* There's nothing in there about restrictions. Or cutting down. Or eating nothing but grapefruit for a week. "Food and drink regularly consumed" sounds like something you should be able to do forever. And with *Lighten Up,* you can. Because an automatic diet is a way of eating you can live with—not just for a few weeks but always.

A trendy diet, on the other hand, is anything but regular.

THE NAKED TRUTH ABOUT TRENDY DIETS

Q: If trendy diets are so bad, why are they so popular? I know lots of people who've lost weight using them. Why can't I do it, too?

A: *The truth is, trendy diets do work…for a while.*

These diets can actually help you lose weight in the first week or two. Some of them may even work for months. And it's the same for all the big diets you know of:

- **The diet restricts your food.** You're probably thinking, "Duh!" But what you may not realize is, this applies to *all* diets—whether they're high-protein, low-carb, low-fat, raw foods, macrobiotic, vegetarian, French, or *whatever.*

That means…

- **You have fewer choices.** Naturally, this tricks you into cutting calories.
- **You lose weight.** Because you're cutting calories. (More on calories later!)
- **You get bored** and start wishing you could eat those "forbidden" foods.
- **You give up** and eventually gain the weight back.

Now, if that's not bad enough, here's the real, bottom-line catch-22 of trendy dieting:

- The faster you lose weight, the more likely you are to keep going with a diet. (That's what all the studies say...and it makes sense, right?)

BUT

- The studies also say that the faster you lose weight, the more likely you are to gain it back.

Ironic, huh? And if you don't believe the studies, just look around you. You'll see what I mean. The simple fact is, any diet that works *at lightning speed* (the way trendy diets promise) is almost impossible to stick with—because it restricts your life and your eating habits way too much.

SO WHY THE CARB CRAZE?

Like any other trendy diet, low-carb diets ask you to cut down on certain types of foods (in this case, anything with a "high" carb count). When you narrow down your food choices, you narrow down what you eat. So you consume fewer calories.

Believe it or not, **most of these diets aren't even *meant* to last!** I'm not kidding. These diets are actually designed for quick results that disappear just as quickly. A quick fix is the easiest way to get you to buy into the hype!

I don't know about you, but this *does not* sound like much of a fix. Do you know anyone who wants to lose weight *and* gain it back?!

Another Trendy Diet Letdown

With trendy diets, much of the "weight you're losing" is often *not* fat but water and lean muscle.

Who cares, as long as you lose the weight, right?

But wait a second. When you lose muscle, your **metabolism** slows down. And that's the *last* thing you want for your body, because it'll cause you to gain weight again very soon. It's the diet yo-yo in full effect!

Q: I don't really care about a few months down the road, as long as I lose weight now. So why does all this matter?

A: Well, think about it. If it's uncomfortable to be overweight, how uncomfortable is it going to be to lose that weight and then gain it back? Why go to the trouble, when you can have an automatic diet that's *easier* than a trendy, quick-fix diet—and that keeps the weight off for good?

Metabolism

The way your body processes the stuff you eat. The slower it is, the easier it is for you to gain weight.

WHY THE CRASH AND BURN?

Okay, I've told you the technical reason why trendy diets are a huge letdown. But there's an even bigger reason lurking on the horizon. The fact is, trendy diets can't work…because they're created by somebody else! By somebody who doesn't know anything about you.

They Forgot Your Genes!

Circle whether the statement is true or false *for you.*

1. My parents are overweight and so am I: T   F

2. I have been overweight since I can remember: T   F

3. My friends can eat the same amount as me,
   but I'm the one who gains weight: T   F

If you answered "true" to one or all of these questions, it's likely that being overweight is at least partly in your genes. Think about it. We all know someone who can eat and eat and eat and gain no weight at all. We also know someone (like, maybe, ourselves) who eats normal amounts of food and is stuck with extra pounds that seem to have come out of nowhere.

The fact is, many overweight people consume no more calories than people who are not overweight. Scientists have known for a while that genes play a big part in our weight. In other words, it's not about being lazy or lacking willpower.

It's also not about giving up. Are you suddenly thinking, "It's in my genes—game over"?

Sorry, you won't get off the hook that easily. Genes are a *factor.* But that's just another one of the problems with a one-size-fits-all approach:

They Forgot Your Life!

Another thing one-size-fits-all diets fail to nail is that your life isn't designed carb-free or fat-free. I doubt you have the time to obsess over calorie counts, or that your parents give you an allowance for specially prepared meals. It's not that easy to find low-carb items at your school cafeteria, or even in the pantry at home.

Chances are you've been in plenty of situations where sticking to a "diet" without going hungry wasn't even an option. The truth is, you eat what's around you—out of habit, or because it's what you've always done, or because there's simply no other choice. Your environment has a big influence on your weight.

THE EMBARRASSMENT FACTOR

Will your friends laugh if you order a slice of pizza with light cheese? Will you get teased if you jog around your neighborhood? Will the waitress smirk if you order a salad with dressing on the side?

I'm going to help you to design a diet that's embarrassment-free. That means plenty of *real* suggestions that'll help you keep your diet private, if that's what you want. For example:

- You may not want to jump rope in your driveway, but would you do it in your basement?
- You may not be willing to order herbal tea at Starbucks, but can you deal with a skim mocha latte?
- You may not want to order a McSalad Shaker at McDonald's, but what about a Chicken McGrill without the bun and no mayo?

You'll see—it can be easy to keep weight loss under wraps for as long as you want.

The Starvation Trap

TRUE OR FALSE

It's good to stay hungry when you're on a diet. It means you're doing something right. After all, no pain, no gain. T or F

If you answered "true" to the previous statement, here's a fact that may shock you: Not only is going hungry not fun— **it's bad for your diet.**

That's because the body's got an ancient survival mechanism that works against starvation. Your body doesn't know that you are cutting down on food *on purpose.* When it senses that you're taking in fewer calories, it thinks you're starving, *literally.* So, to keep you from shedding "valuable" fat, it tries to preserve the calories you are consuming by slowing down your metabolism. Basically, holding onto those calories— and really, those pounds—is your body's way of defending itself against starvation.

To make matters worse, when you starve yourself, your *brain* gets in on the body's conspiracy. The more you try not to eat, the more your brain (along with your body) defends its desire to eat. Again, it's a survival thing, and it's been thousands of years in the making. It's not going to change any time soon.

This book will give you the skills to make your metabolism work *for* your diet, not against it.

Diet Downfalls

In addition to genes, physical surroundings, and your body's survival tactics, a huge piece of any diet is mental. That's another thing quick and trendy diets forget. Sure, it would be fine to give up carbs forever, *if giving up carbs forever didn't make you want them so darn badly!* I'm sure you've been in plenty of situations where you intended to stay away from a box of cookies, or steer clear of pizza, or pass up that next hamburger. But it's not that simple! You *crave* it—and it's not just you, it's everyone. I call these cravings, along with a few other mental factors, diet downfalls.

Here's a list of them. Check off the ones you've experienced:

❏ **The Post-Diet High:** As soon as you lose weight, the first thing you do is gorge on all the foods (good and bad) that were off-limits. *"Now that I'm thin, I can eat anything!"*

❏ **Diet-Failure Despair:** As soon as you realize the diet isn't working the way you expected, you feel so disappointed that you give up. *"I might as well go for it—my diet's not working anyway."*

❏ **The Energy Zap:** You get burnt out by all the time and effort your diet requires. *"I'm really tired of this. I can't do it anymore."*

❏ **The Craving Crazies:** You obsess over the food you're not allowed to have, and then you overeat. *"I've given up ice cream, but now it's all I can think about."*

Jot a Lot

Remember to keep your notebook handy! As you read, jot down anything that seems like it'll fit with your lifestyle. Ask yourself, "Can I do this forever?" If the answer seems like it might be yes, get it on paper.

The way you think and feel about food and your diet matters…*a lot.* That's why this book deals with the mental *and* physical sides of dieting. You're about to create a diet (really a way of eating—remember, we're not talking about restrictions here!) that doesn't force you to *think* about what you're missing. Believe me, it's doable.

WHAT YOU JUST GOT

In this step, you've discovered why so many diets work in the short run (by reducing calories) and why they fail in the long run (they don't fit who you are—physically or mentally). You know the dismal success rates of most diets. And you've heard my promise that this book will put you ahead of the game.

As you move along the next nine steps, you'll get everything you need to avoid becoming one of the 98% of people who fail at their diets, and join the 2% who triumph. You'll do it by building a diet that's so much a part of your everyday life, it'll be automatic.

NEXT UP

You've got the basics, now make it a reality! Step 2 will show you a new way to eat—without giving up the foods you can't live without.

STEP 2 Make It Real

This step is about finding Calorie Bargains—and creating a livable diet. And don't worry, because I'm not going to tell you to count calories for the rest of your life. And I'm not going to ask you to memorize a bunch of facts. I'm just going to show you how to recognize Calorie Bargains and Calorie Rip-offs—and make the latter a thing of the past.

→ Even your smallest food choices matter more than you might think.

GET TO KNOW YOUR CALORIE BARGAINS

Pay attention. This is actually the most important concept in this book, because it's **these tiny trade-offs** that are going to make your dream weight happen and last forever. Also, because I know you're probably pretty busy, this step will give you a list of instant Calorie Bargains you can use at school, at home, or when you're eating out with your friends.

Calorie Bargain: when you trade a fattening food for an equally satisfying, less-fattening one.

Every one of your bargains needs to be designed to be delicious, satisfying, and simple. Let me say it again: *delicious, satisfying, simple.* It's **very important** that you like what you're eating. Because that's the key to making it last forever.

So let's get on with it!

THE THREE-DAY FOOD CHALLENGE

A Three-Day Food Challenge? Wait! What about those Calorie Bargains?

We're getting there. But to figure out how to make small changes in the way you eat, we've got to pin down *how you eat already.* We need to figure out your comfort zone. Here's a visual of what I mean:

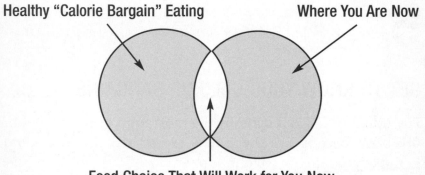

Healthy "Calorie Bargain" Eating   Where You Are Now

Food Choice That Will Work for You Now

For your diet to be automatic, it's got to be comfortable—it's got to be somewhere between the circle on the left and the circle on the right. It has to be in *the middle zone*—where you're comfortable and satisfied but also at the weight you want to be.

That's where the Three-Day Food Challenge comes in. It isn't much of a challenge, actually—because all I'm going to ask you to do is continue eating the way you always do for the next three days. The only difference is that I want you to write down what you eat.

What's in It for Me?

If you're thinking, "Why bother?" I hear you. It might be a hassle to keep track of everything you put in your mouth for the next few days, and if you want to skip it, you can. But before you do, here's why the Three-Day Food Challenge is so helpful:

- It will help you scout out the high-calorie foods you could stand to lose.

- If you're like most people, you have food habits—like late-night snacking—that you don't even notice. Your three-day food diary will reveal what those habits are.

Are You Up for It?

If you're still not interested, my suggestion is to write down the foods you've eaten over the past three days, from memory. But beware: Most people underestimate how much they eat. So if you're not sure whether you had five potato chips or twenty, lean on the side of twenty—it's probably more accurate. (You can always use a camera phone to photograph everything you eat and record it at the end of the day.)

Whether you're tackling the challenge over three days or only over the next few minutes of memory-writing, go ahead and get started.

_____

_____

_____

_____

_____

_____

_____

Taking the Three-Day Food Challenge

How to take the challenge:

1. Eat as you normally would for the next three days.
2. Record what you eat for all three days by filling in the blanks provided.

P.S. If you forget this book, or don't feel like carrying it around, just keep your notebook handy and write your diary entry there. If all you can dig up is a spare slip of paper, you can staple it into your notebook later.

When you write down what you eat, write down *how much* of it you eat. Three pieces? A handful? If you have the package your food came in, you can get started on some early basic label-reading by checking out the serving size under Nutrition Facts and writing down how many servings you've had. For example, a serving of Kellogg's Frosted Flakes is ¾ cup. Did you have that much? Twice that much? Almost everyone eats more than the listed serving size, so make sure to be honest. It's important to get this info right; otherwise, the calories, fat, carbs, and protein you're counting won't add up to the real amount.

Here's a sample Three-Day Food Challenge from Jen, age fifteen.

What you ate: *3 small pieces fried chicken; salad with blue cheese dressing; can of Coke (740 calories)*
Where you ate: *Cafeteria*
When you ate: *Lunchtime, 12:30 P.M.*
Why you ate: *Lunch/Hungry*
How you felt: *Gross after eating fried food*

What you ate: *1 package Reese's Peanut Butter Cups; a normal-size glass of 2% milk. (372 calories)*
Where you ate: *Home*
When you ate: *4:30-ish*

Why you ate: *Bored and craving chocolate*
How you felt: *Happy. I'm a chocolate fiend.*

What you ate: *Big bowl of fettuccine Alfredo
    (1,150 calories)*
Where you ate: *Home*
When you ate: *6-ish*
Why you ate: *Dinner*
How you felt: *Stuffed*

Other meals and snacks: *Around 9:00 P.M. I
    had 3 handfuls of dry Fruity Pebbles while
    I was watching TV, because I wanted
    something sweet. I felt more awake after-
    wards. (110 calories)*

- Make sure to keep track of *any* and *all* snacks: Eating chips in front of the TV counts! So do one or two Hershey's Kisses or pieces of candy.
- If you want to check the serving size but don't have a package, you can get the info on freshdirect.com (if they ask for your zip code, just put in 10011). It's an online food delivery service in New York, but you can use it to get all sorts of info on the foods you eat.

DAY 1

What you ate: _____
Where you ate: _____
When you ate: _____
Why you ate: _____
How you felt: _____

What you ate: _____
Where you ate: _____
When you ate: _____
Why you ate: _____
How you felt: _____

What you ate: _____
Where you ate: _____
When you ate: _____
Why you ate: _____
How you felt: _____

Other meals and snacks: _____

DAY 2

What you ate: _____
Where you ate: _____
When you ate: _____
Why you ate: _____
How you felt: _____

What you ate: _____
Where you ate: _____
When you ate: _____
Why you ate: _____
How you felt: _____

What you ate: _____
Where you ate: _____
When you ate: _____
Why you ate: _____
How you felt: _____

Other meals and snacks: _____

DAY 3

What you ate: _____
Where you ate: _____
When you ate: _____
Why you ate: _____
How you felt: _____

Q: Why should I write *why* I'm eating? Isn't it obvious?

A: Hunger is only one of the reasons we eat. We also eat when we're stressed, bored, lonely, nervous.... It helps to know *why* you eat when you're trying to change the *way* you eat. Maybe you can see a pattern.

What you ate: _____

Where you ate: _____

When you ate: _____

Why you ate: _____

How you felt: _____

What you ate: _____

Where you ate: _____

When you ate: _____

Why you ate: _____

How you felt: _____

Other meals and snacks: _____

You've Taken the Challenge. Now What?

Quickly glance through your diary. Were there any surprises? Do you eat more candy than you thought you did? Do you eat four servings of cereal for breakfast instead of one? (You wouldn't be the only one.) Do you snack a lot more than you ever suspected? The idea is to examine your food diary—or the foods you eat on a regular basis—and then see where you could compromise.

For instance, if you typically eat ice cream four nights a week, and it's the highest-calorie version, you've got an opportunity to find a great Calorie Bargain. Go to the supermarket (join one of your parents on a trip if you don't drive) and look for a few lower-cal ice creams you think you could love. Then buy one or more at a time, depending on your budget. If you get one home and it doesn't satisfy you, try another kind the next time. Hopefully, you'll hit on one that tastes great and costs fewer

Just finding three or four Calorie Bargains like this could help you lose twenty pounds or more in one year—effortlessly and painlessly!

calories. But even if you don't, scoping out your food diary will help you find other possible bargains.

You see, you don't need to deprive yourself at all. It's all about compromise.

MEET YOUR NUTRITION LABEL

Before you know how to use it, you've got to know how to read it. Try picking an item from your food diary—something you have the package for. How many calories does it have? Don't forget to multiply by the number of servings you had. Write it down below:

Nutrition Facts		
Serving Size 1 cup (228g)		
Servings Per Container 2		

Amount Per Serving		
Calories 260	Calories from Fat 120	

		% Daily Value*
Total Fat 13g		**20%**
Saturated Fat 5g		**25%**
Trans Fat 2g		
Cholesterol 30mg		**10%**
Sodium 660mg		**28%**
Total Carbohydrate 31g		**10%**
Dietary Fiber 0g		**0%**
Sugars 5g		
Protein 5g		

Vitamin A 4%	•	Vitamin C 2%
Calcium 15%	•	Iron 4%

*Percent Daily Values are based on a 2,000 calorie diet. Your Daily Values may be higher or lower depending on your calorie needs:

	Calories:	2,000	2,500
Total Fat	Less than	65g	80g
Sat Fat	Less than	20g	25g
Cholesterol	Less than	300mg	300mg
Sodium	Less than	2,400mg	2,400mg
Total Carbohydrate		300g	375g
Dietary Fiber		25g	30g

Calories per gram:
Fat 9 • Carbohydrate 4 • Protein 4

An example from Jen's food diary:

What you ate: *3 pieces of fried chicken*

Calories: *130 calories per serving x 3 (number of servings) = 390 calories*

What you ate: _____

Calories: _____

What's in a Calorie?

Calories are nothing more than a combination of fats (9 calories per gram), carbohydrates (4 calories per gram), and protein (4 calories per gram). So, if something has 21 calories, it could have 1 fat gram (9 calories), 2 grams of carbohydrates (8 calories), and 1 gram of protein (4 calories). That's how it all works. It's that simple.

NOW MAKE IT MAKE SENSE...AND LIGHTEN UP

Okay. Now that you know how to figure out the calories, fat, carbs, and protein you're consuming, here's the skinny on what it all means....

Calories Count

First of all, you need to know that calories are more important than carbs, protein, or fat. Now, I've got some good news and some bad news for you. The bad news is that it doesn't take a whole lot of extra calories to pack on the pounds. The good news is that it works the other way, too. Cutting even 100 calories out of your day—using your food label as a guide—can really make a difference in your weight.

If you really want to boost your label knowledge, try adding up the calories of a whole meal, or a whole day's worth of meals, in your notebook. It'll help you spot places where the food turns out to be more fattening than it's worth.

So how do you know what a good Calorie Bargain is and which calories to cut? Use these basic guidelines and it'll be a no-brainer. Once you know how to make these simple compromises, it'll become so easy, it'll be automatic:

How Much Exercise Does It Take to Work Off Extra Calories?
5 Hershey's Chocolate Kisses = about 15 minutes of running
One Oreo Double Stuf cookie = about 18 minutes of swimming laps
One McDonald's Big Mac; large fries; large Coke = about 7 hours of dog-walking

Fill Yourself Up

When you're looking for Calorie Bargains, it's not enough to just pick lower-calorie foods. The real key is finding low-calorie foods that will **also** keep you full.

Q: How do I know what will keep me full?

A: Use What You Know: Make a mental note of the foods that seem to keep your belly satisfied without costing you a ton of calories. Once you notice what these foods are, you'll have them on mental file for later.

Got Water? Look for foods with a high water content. Wondering which ones those are?

Vegetables, fruits, and whole grains contain lots of water, which means you get to eat more and gain less (less calories, less fat, less weight).

MORE WAYS TO FILL UP

Protein Power: Foods that are high in protein and low in fat (example: boneless chicken breast) keep you full and help you build lean muscle.

Sow Your Oats: Real, whole-oat oatmeal—not the instant kind that comes in packets—is easy to get, easy to make, and sticks with you much longer than waffles or sugary cereal.

Add It Up: Try adding blueberries to your cereal, veggies to your pizza, or ask your mom to add eggplant to her lasagna—you'll be adding extra food without a bunch of extra calories.

Magic Soup: Because it's packed with water, soup fills you up. And having a cup of the right soup before a meal will help you eat less afterward. Not to mention, it's easy to ask your mom or dad to pick up at the store, and easy to prepare.

Compare Labels

Comparing one nutrition label to another is one of the best ways to find out where you can save on calories. Comparing labels gives you the chance to make a choice: "Are the extra 160 calories really worth it for a Coke instead of a Diet Coke? Would I be just as happy with a piece of homemade tomato-veggie pizza as with this way-more-fattening slice of double-cheese-and-sausage pizza?" If the Diet Coke and the cheeseless pizza work for you, you've saved about 375 calories! On the other hand, if only the Red Baron pizza will do, fine. Comparing labels for calorie deals and steals will help you find other ways to save.

Never eat anything with more than 200 calories without taking five seconds to decide if it's really worth it. Is it a Calorie Bargain or a Calorie Rip-off?

Automatic Calorie Deals and Steals

No time to make your own Calorie Bargains? The ready-made ones listed below are fantastic—simple, tasty, and great for your shape. Check off the ones that sound doable to you so you can refer to them when you need quick and easy ideas. You can also copy (or tear out) this page, chop it up, and stick the different sections on your fridge and inside your locker as an extra reminder.

Keep in mind that the best Calorie Bargains are the ones you make yourself. It only takes a minute or two to investigate and decide. But the savings last forever.

MEALS		
Instead of	Try	You Saved
Spaghetti and (beef) meatballs, 3 cups (770 calories)	Spaghetti and turkey meatballs, 3 cups (630 calories)	140 calories
Cheese pizza, 1 medium slice (280 calories)	Pita bread pizza with skim mozzarella (216 calories)	64 calories
Beef stir-fry with fat-free cooking spray (260 calories)	Shrimp and vegetable stir-fry with fat-free cooking spray (200 calories)	60 calories

Watch out for liquid Calorie Rip-offs. Even 100% juice has major calories. Think about it: Five or six oranges had to be squeezed to make that one glass of juice—so you're getting the sugar from all those oranges.

Also, make sure to keep calorie-free beverages like sparkling or regular water, diet soda, and unsweetened iced tea on your family's grocery list.

TREATS		
Instead of	Try	You Saved
Brownies, 2 oz. (227 calories)	Fat-free chocolate pudding, ½ cup (130 calories)	97 calories
Regular vanilla ice cream, 1 cup (280 calories)	Light vanilla ice cream, 1 cup (200 calories)	80 calories

DRINKS		
Instead of	Try	You Saved
Tropicana Pure Premium Grovestand orange juice, 8-oz. glass (110 calories)	Tropicana Light 'n Healthy orange juice, 8-oz. glass (70 calories)	40 calories
Arizona lemonade, 15.5-oz. can (110 calories)	Homemade unsweetened iced tea with Splenda (0 calories)	110 calories
Coke, 12-oz. can (160 calories)	Diet Coke, 12-oz. can (0 calories)	160 calories
Lemon-lime Gatorade, 8-oz. glass (50 calories)	Water with a slice of lemon (8 calories)	42 calories

If you replace one 12-ounce soda with a diet soda each day, you'll drop more than 15 pounds in one year!

BLOT A LOT

Cut down on the fat by blotting your French fries, pizza slice, or hamburger meat with a napkin before you eat it. Blotting your pizza can save as many as 80 calories! If your friends think it's weird, just tell them you think all that grease is nasty. After all, these tiny habits result in a major payoff!

At the Snack Machine

Don't go into "king-size denial": The snacks I've listed come in regular-size packages. Don't forget that if you choose king-size, the calories will become king-size, too.

SALTY TREATS		
Instead of	Try	You Saved
Cheetos, 1-oz. bag (160 calories)	Pretzels/Rold Gold Classic Tiny Twists, 1-oz. bag (110 calories)	50 calories
Doritos, 1-oz. bag (140 calories)	Baked Lays, 1-oz. bag (110 calories)	30 calories
Combos, 1.8-oz bag (240 calories)	Peanuts 1.75-oz. bag (220 calories)	20 calories

SWEET TREATS		
Instead of	Try	You Saved
Peanut M&Ms, regular-size bag (250 calories)	Stick of gum (10 calories)	240 calories
Snickers, regular-size (250 calories)	Nature Valley Granola Bars, package of two (180 calories)	70 calories

COOKIES AND BAKED STUFF		
Instead of	Try	You Saved
Kellogg's frosted cherry Pop-Tarts, package of two (408 calories)	Rice Krispie Treat (200 calories)	208 calories
Famous Amos peanut butter cookies, 2-oz. bag (260 calories)	Fig Newtons, 2-oz. package (200 calories)	60 calories

Beverage Dos and Don'ts
Dos: Water, diet soda, diet iced tea
Don'ts: Regular soda, fruit "drinks" (like Fruitopia)

AT THE MOVIES

These days, a large buttered popcorn with soda and a bag of candy could add up to as much as 2,500 calories and more than three days' worth of saturated fat. Even if you go to the movies *only* once a month, you could gain as much as 8.5 pounds a year.

Here are some tips for brave audience members ready to break the concession stand "addiction" cycle:

Sneak Attack: You may be telling yourself, well, if my theater would just let me bring my own food from home, I wouldn't eat so badly. Well, some theaters have a "don't ask, don't tell" policy when it comes to bringing in healthy snacks—meaning they're not going to check your bag or police the aisles looking for your baggie of chopped-up red pepper sticks. Bring in foods that don't smell and won't get crushed when they're shoved in your bag. Focus on foods that are very low-cal—so that you can mindlessly munch on them throughout the movie, just like popcorn.

Try:

- **Homemade air-popped popcorn:** At only 30 calories per cup, it's a good deal.

- **Cereal:** Kashi (a variety of healthy versions) or Cheerios are both low-calorie choices that are pretty durable.

- **Beef jerky**

- **Fruit:** Apples are not easily crushed when hidden in your bag. It's a good idea to cut them into slices.

- **Rice cakes:** Watch the calorie and fat content.

- **Energy bars:** These are a bit better than those king-size chocolate bars.

Eat Before: What a novel idea! Stuff yourself with low-calorie healthy foods before you actually go to the movies so you just can't eat another bite.

The Best of the Worst: If you must eat at the concession stand, focus on limiting the total calories of food or candy. It's misleading to just look at the calories per serving on the food label—how many of us actually count out one serving and put the rest away? In all likelihood, you'll eat the whole package, no matter how many people you say you're going to share it with.

Just take a look at the movie-size version of Reese's Pieces (8 oz.), which has a whopping 1,200 calories, 60 grams of fat, and 138 grams of carbs. How about those Twizzlers? They look tempting with their claim, "As Always, a Low-Fat Candy," but the 6-ounce package holds 600 calories, 4 grams of fat, and 136 grams of carbs. And that bag of Skittles might look like a healthier option, with only 2 grams of fat per serving, but the 6.75-ounce bag has 765 calories, 9 grams of fat, and 166.5 grams of carbs.

CALORIES FOR SOME OF OUR FAVORITE MOVIE CANDY

Goobers (3.5 oz.): 525 calories, 35g fat, 55g carbs

Gummi Bears (4 oz.): 390 calories, 0g fat, 90g carbs

Junior Mints (3 oz.): 320 calories, 5g fat, 68g carbs

M&M's (5.3 oz.): 735 calories, 31.5g fat, 105g carbs

Milk Duds (3 oz.): 340 calories, 12g fat, 56g carbs

Raisinets (3.5 oz.): 380 calories, 16g fat, 64g carbs

Reese's Pieces (8 oz.): 1,200 calories, 60g fat, 138g carbs

Skittles (6.75 oz.): 765 calories, 9g fat, 166.5g carbs

Sno-Caps (3.1 oz.): 360 calories, 16g fat, 60g carbs

Twizzlers Strawberry Twists (6 oz.): 600 calories, 4g fat, 136g carbs

Calorie Bargains Gone Bad—for Replacement Only

Balance Bars

They've got 200 calories, 6 grams of fat, and 22 grams of carbs. Just to compare, a Snickers bar has 280 calories, 14 grams of fat, and 35 grams of carbs. So, yes, if you eat Snickers bars on a regular basis, a Balance Bar is a Calorie Bargain. *But,* if you don't normally eat candy bars, and you *start* to eat Balance Bars or PowerBars, you're actually gaining calories.

Frozen Yogurt

Just because it's low- or nonfat doesn't mean it's calorie-free! It's usually got a lot of sugar, and often this "healthy" treat's got as many calories as ice cream. Check the label! If you're not using it as a replacement for something higher in fat, you're not doing yourself any favors by adding it to your diet!

Veggie Chips and Other Health Food Snacks

Same thing. They make a good substitute for fattier junk food, but don't think you can binge without gaining weight!

Nuts

They're an important part of a healthy diet and they're packed with protein, but don't go crazy on them—they have loads of calories. If you munch, go for a handful of maybe five or six, not a whole bag or can. And remember, the idea is to substitute them for other, less healthy and filling options.

Potential Calorie Rip-offs

Slim-Fast

A can of dark chocolate fudge–flavor Slim-Fast has 220 calories—more than a can of Yoo-hoo and more than twice as many as a can of Yoo-hoo Lite. Sure, the Slim-Fast's got more nutrients and is more filling, but if you're just looking for a tasty, chocolaty drink, it's a major Calorie Rip-off! It's supposed to replace an entire meal, not be a drink.

Dried Fruit

It's high in calories because it's packed with sugar. Eat real fruit—it's more filling and a better deal caloriewise.

See why it's so helpful to read the label? Calorie Bargains— and Calorie Rip-offs—are lurking in the most surprising places. And now you know how to find them.

Now That You Know...

I'm not saying that you shouldn't eat this stuff. In fact, this book will never say you *shouldn't* eat anything—you can make that decision for yourself! But it's important to know what you're getting so that:

- You don't overdo it, thinking you can eat as much of these foods as you want without gaining weight. Even healthy foods are not "free" foods.
- You don't make the wrong sacrifices—like eating frozen yogurt instead of ice cream—for the wrong reasons. (If you *love* ice cream and you aren't crazy about frozen yogurt, you might be depriving yourself for no reason!)

But being a bargain hunter doesn't stop there. Cutting calories is the key to cutting weight, it's true. But to get the best food bargains, and make them automatic, you need to know a little about fats and carbs, too.

THE SKINNY ON FATS

Fat gets a bad rap. We *need* some fat in our diet to stay healthy, energized, satisfied, and feeling full. In fact, we need about 25% to 30% of our calorie intake to come from fat. The problem is, many of us eat a lot more than that.

Fat gets all the attention it does from nutritionists because it's "expensive." What does that mean? It means a little fat packs a lot of calories—which makes it easy for us to rack up weight without eating all that much.

And here's something even more important: You need to know what kind of fat you're eating. Yep, there are *types* of fats—some that are good for you and some that aren't. And sticking to the *good* kind will help you look *and* feel great. Here's a list.

Good Fats vs. Evil Fats

EVIL FATS

Saturated Fat *Found in:* Meat, whole-milk dairy products, poultry skin, egg yolks

Trans Fat *Found in:* Margarines, shortenings, fast food. Also in store-bought pies, cookies, cakes, and crackers. Look for the words *partially hydrogenated oil* on the ingredients list, and that's your biggest clue that you have trans fat.

GOOD FATS

Monounsaturated *Found in:* Canola, peanut, and olive oils; peanuts; avocados

Polyunsaturated *Found in:* Sunflower, corn, safflower, cottonseed, and soybean oils; nuts; fish

Q: Is butter better than margarine?

A: Typically margarine is the better choice, but make sure it has no trans fats—the package often says "trans fat–free" right on the label. Stick margarine still contains unhealthy trans fat, but many tubs and sprays don't.

Now That You Know...

You don't have to know how to pronounce them, and you don't have to avoid evil fats like the plague. It's good to keep an eye out for them, though, when you're reading labels or choosing your foods. Pretty soon you'll know what to watch out for automatically.

Remember that even though "good" fat can be healthy, too much will make you gain weight no matter what.

Some Easy Ideas for Trimming the Fat (and Calories)!

- Soy chips instead of potato chips
- Baked, steamed, or grilled foods instead of fried
- Light, healthy, or reduced-fat versions (example: light sour cream instead of regular; low-fat mayo instead of regular). Remember, you need to check the label, because not all reduced- or nonfat foods are lower in calories.

THE FRONT LABEL

Here are a few hints that will help you to avoid Calorie Rip-offs and hunt for the Calorie Bargains when you're dealing with the labels on the *front* of your foods:

The Food and Drug Administration (FDA) regulates the use of these terms, but the front of the food label can be as complicated to read as the back!

Fat-Free: For a food to be labeled "fat-free," it's got to have less than 0.5 grams of fat *per serving.* The key words here are per serving! Remember that the serving size may be quite different from the amount you actually eat! And don't forget that many fat-free foods have almost as many calories as similar foods that are not fat-free—usually because the fat has been replaced with additional sugar.

Low-Fat: To qualify as low-fat, a food must contain 3 grams of fat or less per serving. (Notice those words again—*per serving.*) But that doesn't mean it's necessarily healthy or low in calories.

Reduced or Less Fat: To qualify as a reduced-fat food, the product must have at least 25% less fat per serving than the original version. If you see a "reduced-fat" claim, be wary—yes, it's reduced, but the question is, *from what?* Don't ever assume that because the label says "reduced fat" you can eat larger portions without adding extra calories.

Sugar-Free: When you see this on the front of the label, it means that the product has less than 0.5 grams of sugar per serving. But again, that doesn't mean it's necessarily healthy or great for weight loss.

No Sugar Added: "No added sugars" and "without added sugars" claims mean that no sugar or sugar-containing ingredient (like fruit juices, applesauce, or dried fruit) is added during processing or packing. Pay attention, though, because it doesn't mean the food is low-calorie or reduced-calorie or even sugar-free.

Light: A "light" food is one that has one-third fewer calories *or* half the fat of a previous version of the food. Remember to ask the question: How many calories—or how much fat—did it have before?

This label can also be confusing because "light" can be used to refer to the color or texture of the product—not just its fat or calorie content. Light olive oil, for example, contains the same amount of fat as any other olive oil—nearly 14 grams per tablespoon.

CARBS NEED LOVE, TOO

Maybe you've heard your parents talk about them as if they were poison or your friends discuss them at lunch with mingled fear and horror. Maybe you too have joined in the persecution of carbs—avoiding them at every meal.

It's all too bad, considering that carbohydrates are important to our survival. High-carb foods include such suspicious items as fruits, vegetables, beans, nuts, milk, and yogurt. Of course, they also include "bad" foods such as cakes, sodas, cookies, and sugar.

Here are the facts on the nation's most misunderstood nutrient:

First, carbs can be explained by looking at two carb nutrients: **dietary fiber** and **sugar.** Before you start to doze off at the words *dietary fiber,* just know this: It's the category of carb that keeps you full and energized longer. The second category of carbs, sugars, are actually naturally found in food—but most of the sugar you hear about is *added,* often in the form of high-fructose corn syrup.

When you're losing weight (or keeping it off) and dealing with carbs, you should go for foods that are high in fiber—like the whole grains, vegetables, and fruit I discussed earlier. Here's why: **High-fiber foods help you lose weight because they fill up your stomach without filling you up with extra calories.** They also take a long time to digest—so you *stay* full.

In case you were wondering...
Fiber in food helps to fill you up. Fiber in pills doesn't.

Q: Are seven-grain and multigrain breads better for you than 100% whole wheat?

A: No, they're not. One hundred percent whole grains have been associated with health benefits like losing weight and reducing the risk of your getting certain diseases. But most multigrain breads aren't 100%. Check the Nutrition Facts panel. If the first ingredient isn't some sort of whole grain, you are not getting 100% benefits.

THE BIG PICTURE

Now that you have the scoop on carbs, fat, and calories, you're ready for some serious food bargain–hunting.

You can find a Calorie Bargain in just three easy steps.

Step 1: Think of a food you typically eat each day. It might be a guilty pleasure or simply a food you eat that's very high in calories but that you think might be worth losing...*if* you had a good substitute.

> *Example*
>
> The food I eat now that I'm willing to change: *Lay's regular potato chips*
>
> Serving size I would eat in a typical sitting (Be honest!): *3 servings (about 4 handfuls)*
>
> Okay, now my total calories: 150 x 3 = 450 calories

Step 2: Now try to think of a substitute for that food you usually eat. It's got to be one you at least think you might like, and it's got to have fewer calories.

> *Example*
>
> My potential Calorie Bargain (food I will try switching to): Air-popped popcorn
>
> Serving size I would probably eat in a typical sitting (Be honest!): 3 servings (about 4 handfuls)
>
> Okay, now my total calories: 75 calories

You just saved a whopping 375 calories. So if you ate chips three times per week, and you replaced them with popcorn... you could lose as much as 15 pounds in a year!

Step 3: Look at how many calories you saved. Is this Calorie Bargain worth it?

Now take a look at your Three-Day Food Challenge and use the worksheet below to come up with three Calorie Bargains of your own.

1. The food I eat now that I'm willing to substitute: _____

   _____

   Serving size I would eat in a typical sitting: _____

   _____

   Total calories: _____

   My potential Calorie Bargain: _____

   _____

   Serving size I would probably eat in a typical sitting: ___

   _____

   Total calories: _____

   How many calories I saved by making the switch: _____

   Rate It Is this a good choice? Why do I think it will or won't last? _____

   _____

2. The food I eat now that I'm willing to substitute: _____

   _____

   Serving size I would eat in a typical sitting: _____

   _____

   Total calories: _____

   My potential Calorie Bargain: _____

   _____

Make an ongoing list of additional Calorie Bargains in your notebook. You should be able to find lots.

Serving size I would probably eat in a typical sitting: ___

_____

Total calories:_____

How many calories I saved by making the switch:_____

Rate It Is this a good choice? Why do I think it will or won't last?_____

_____

3. The food I eat now that I'm willing to substitute: _____

_____

Serving size I would eat in a typical sitting: _____

_____

Total calories:_____

My potential Calorie Bargain: _____

_____

Serving size I would probably eat in a typical sitting: ___

_____

Total calories:_____

How many calories I saved by making the switch:_____

Rate It Is this a good choice? Why do I think it will or won't last?_____

_____

True or False: White chicken meat is healthier than dark chicken meat.

_____

True. White meat is lower in fat than dark meat. And either meat is much lower in fat if you remove the skin.

IT'S ROUTINE!

If you think there's no way counting *every calorie you eat* will become automatic...you're right. People who lose weight forever simply get to know the *kinds* of foods (low in fat, high in fiber, lots of fruits and vegetables) they need to eat to fill themselves up and keep their energy up while keeping their weight down. They do a little work in the beginning—a little label-reading, a little bargain-hunting—and then they reap the rewards. Pretty soon it's automatic.

WHAT YOU JUST GOT

Now that you know what you're looking for, reading labels will only take a second. All you've gotta do is:

- Look for calorie deals and steals.
- Watch out for high fat content—especially if they're bad fats.
- Go with foods you know are high in fiber and low in calories, whenever possible.

The more you use these simple tactics, the simpler it'll be to spot great Calorie Bargains from a mile away. And you won't have to count grams obsessively, because your food know-how will become automatic, fast. You're already practically an expert!

NEXT UP

It's great to *talk* about Calorie Bargains, but chances are you don't buy the groceries...*or* make the decisions about the menu at your cafeteria...*or* get to be in charge of where you eat every time you and your friends hang out. *Life* can get in the way of your diet!

Don't worry, there's a way to deal. That's where Step 3 comes in.

STEP 3 Get a (Diet-Friendly) Life!

MAKE YOUR LIFE A DIET SAFETY ZONE

You may have heard the saying that the first step in fixing a problem is admitting that it's there. It's scary to admit that we don't have complete control over food. Personally, I like to think that I can ignore a pan of brownies in the kitchen or a tub of ice cream in the freezer. I have my own mind, right?

But the truth is, it's *really, really* difficult.

If you're surrounded by junk food at school and your home is practically an all-you-can-eat buffet of sweets, snacks, and fatty meals, it's hard to resist being a person who eats junk food, sweets, snacks, and fat-packed meals. *Unless,* with a capital *U,* you have a plan.

You can take control by making small changes that will make your life a diet safety zone.

If that sounds impossible, it's not.

LOVE ME, LOVE MY DIET

I used to think that asking for support was really just asking people to act like my "food police"—to watch my every move to make sure I stuck to my diet. Funny, that never worked for me. It took me a long time to realize that I didn't need "food police." What I needed was real support from my family and friends. The kind of support that would help *me* help *myself* lose weight.

Family and Friendly Support

Your family and friends can't make or break your diet, but they can have a *big* impact. Here's how.

How Your Friends and Family Can Help

Their support for your diet can help boost your confidence and give you the extra push you need to get your diet on track. Not to mention, your parents, specifically, have the power to control what foods find their way into your kitchen.

How They Sometimes Don't

Think of some things your family or friends may have said or done to discourage you from losing weight and write them below.

_____

_____

_____

_____

Now look them over. How did these things hinder your diet instead of help it?

Why They Might Not Be Supportive

Your family and friends may not want you to "deprive" yourself by passing up that sugary, buttery birthday cake or those greasy french fries. Or they may be unconsciously trying to sabotage your efforts because they feel bad about their own food choices. They may even feel threatened by the possibility that you'll change.

This can be especially true with friends. If you and your pals have always bonded through junk food, or over your less-than-perfect weight, your new commitment could be intimidating to them.

In any case, if you're like most people, you've discovered that your friends and family aren't quite the perfectly evolved support system you'd love them to be. Here are some easy ways to change that.

The Most Unhelpful Diet "Advice" of All Time

- "It's okay to eat that—it's your birthday/anniversary/the weekend (or any excuse)."
- "You're fine just the way you are."
- "Worrying about your weight is just superficial."

DON'T GET PSYCHED OUT!

Even the most confident people can be hurt by "ego threats"—which is when people you care about voice doubts about you or your abilities. Ego threats come from all over, but the most powerful ones come from the people closest to you, which is why they're so dangerous.

Parents and relatives are notorious for making ego threats: "You'll never be able to lose weight, so why try," or the seemingly less brutal "You look good the way you are—don't bother losing weight." Friends can be the same way. You trust these people, and their comments hurt. And that hurt can drive you to make promises like "I'm going to starve myself and lose forty pounds in two months" or "I'm going to get a supermodel body." On the other hand, they can also give you an excuse to throw in the towel. Giving in to these threats—either by pushing too hard or by giving up—means losing touch with what really matters: your success! Don't let what *other* people think of your goals throw you off track. But make sure to talk to a medical doctor and do your research to make sure you need to lose weight—and that you're really in need of a weight-control program.

Get Your Biggest Fans on Board

Include Them

Try to encourage them (this includes your boyfriend or girl-friend, if you have one) to eat for the greater good, too—*without* preaching. Come up with creative ideas: Instead of the usual trip to T.G.I. Friday's, you might cook dinner with a close friend once a week. Partner with a pal who also wants to lose weight and reward yourselves (with a movie or another non-food treat) for sticking to your new habits. Suggest a healthy family meal that you'll help to cook.... The point is, if you can get your family and friends to think about changing their habits, it will have a positive impact on your own.

My creative ideas for including my crew:

_____

_____

_____

_____

_____

Talk It Out

Your reasons for dieting may seem obvious to you, but when you verbalize them to your friends and family, you are really posting a sign that says: **This is important to me. I need your support.** Let your pals and family members know that the reason you want them on board is that their input has a huge impact on your life. Don't be afraid to butter them up. And be sure to hit all the points that might help to make your case.

Points I might bring up when I talk to family and friends about my diet:

Example: *If I'm happier with my body, I'll be happier in general. Do you really want to deal with me being crabby all the time?*

Example: *Your opinion means so much to me, your support would help a lot.*

_____

_____

_____

_____

_____

_____

_____

Buddy Up

Try to find a "diet buddy" at school, online, or in your neighborhood. This person should be in a similar situation and also trying to lose weight. Share walks, lunches, ideas, your own personal diet triumphs, and pep talks. A few words of encouragement a few times a week can go a long way.

Some people I might consider buddying up with:

_____

_____

_____

_____

_____

The Company You Keep

It also wouldn't hurt to make a few new friends who've got it together when it comes to living and eating healthy. They aren't the same as "diet buddies"—they're just people who inspire you to stay on track because they're so good at it themselves, and who might just share the secrets of their success on a regular basis.

P.S. *I'm not suggesting that you replace the friends you already have.* But having a few good influences around couldn't hurt.

Some health-savvy people I might hang out with more often:

_____

_____

_____

_____

_____

_____

COMMUNITY COUNTS

Look outside your circle of immediate family and friends—for example, look online—to find people who are as committed to losing weight as you are. The fact is, sharing your diet ups and downs with others who are doing the same thing has a number of benefits:

- It gives you a shoulder to lean on and an ear to listen, and that can motivate you. When people are in *the same boat* as you, it's a little easier to believe them when they cheer you on.

- You can share the latest and greatest information, such as a great low-cal snack or a new foolproof diet trick. Read on to learn about a few great ways to create community support.

GET SET FOR SUCCESS

Now that you're well on your way to finding soul support, it's time to get moving. As I mentioned earlier in this step, to make your diet indestructible, you need to take control of your environment. I won't be unrealistic here and tell you that your parents will give you control over what they stock in the kitchen, or that your friends will never drag you to McDonald's. But this section will help you learn how to have a bigger say in the choices that are available to you at home, in school, and when you're out with your friends.

HOME SWEETS HOME

This quiz will help you figure out exactly what kind of home turf you're dealing with.

Kitchen Confidential

What type of kitchen do you have? Circle the letter that's closest to the truth.

1. The fruits and vegetables found in my kitchen are
   a. Everywhere you look
   b. The occasional apple or banana going to waste in the fruit bowl
   c. Nonexistent
2. Cookies, candies, and sweets are
   a. Outlawed in my parents' kitchen
   b. Around if I want them
   c. A staple in our house

3. The beverages in our house are

   a. The basics plus unsweetened iced tea, water, skim milk, diet soda, and/or low-cal drink mixes

   b. Water, milk, orange juice: the basics

   c. Soda, fruit "drinks," and/or chocolate milk

4. The cereals we have are

   a. Ones that say things like "high fiber" and are less than 120 calories per serving

   b. Cereals that "look" healthy but have a lot of sugar (Check the label: The closer to the beginning of the ingredients list you find the word *sugar*, the more of it is in the food.)

   c. Of the Fruit Loops and Cocoa Puffs variety

5. The breads in our kitchen are mostly

   a. 100% whole grain

   b. White breads

   c. Doughnuts

6. As far as dairy products go, we've got

   a. Plenty of low-fat options such as yogurt, milk, and cheese

   b. Normal cheese, yogurt, and milk (not reduced-fat)

   c. A liquid that used to look like milk, but something's growing on it

7. My input into the family's grocery shopping decisions is mostly

   a. Writing down what I want on the list on the fridge and/or helping with the shopping

   b. Asking for a few items that come to mind as the shopper rushes out the door

   c. Rifling through the bags when the food arrives

8. If I ask my parents to let me have more input into what food they buy, they'll

   a. Be excited that I want to make positive changes

   b. Roll their eyes but humor me

   c. Look at me like I've sprouted horns. I'm not *paying* for the food, am I?

How does your kitchen measure up?

Mostly A's: Smooth Sailing

Congrats! Your kitchen is covered as far as healthy options, and if you don't like the ones available, your parents are probably open to hearing your suggestions for new ones. That means if your home isn't quite diet-safe yet, it shouldn't be too hard to get it there. The tips on the following pages will give you an extra push in that direction.

Mostly B's: Dicey Territory

Your home isn't *totally* sabotaging your new, healthy eating habits, but it's not making it easy. Your parents may be willing to accommodate your new food choices, but they're not falling over themselves rolling out the red carpet. And they may not understand why the options they've provided aren't good enough. The Pitch In and Make It Simple sections on page 57 may be especially helpful in bringing them around.

Mostly C's: Bermuda Triangle

There's no denying it—your kitchen is a major danger zone. With so many sweets and fattening foods around, it's no wonder you have a hard time resisting the urge. What's worse, your parents may be unwilling to support your diet—they might even be opposed to it. The Keep the Family Peace section below will be especially helpful to you.

SOS! GETTING YOUR PARENTS (AND YOUR KITCHEN) TO COOPERATE!

Unless you recently inherited a fortune, you probably don't have the money to stock your kitchen yourself. Which means it would be a huge help to get your parents in on the act. Here are a few surefire ways to be heard.

Keep the Family Peace

Sit down with your parents and have a reasoned, rational discussion about why it's important for you to lose weight. Bring up issues that are important to *them*, like your health, your happiness, and your confidence.

Explain that you're not asking them to change their lives, you're just asking for them to understand and support the change in yours. And make sure it's clear that you're not asking them to be your "food police." Explain that you're the one who has to take responsibility for your diet but that their support would mean a lot to you. Hopefully, they'll respect your willingness to take responsibility and put in the extra effort to support you.

What points could I bring up that would help my family give their support?

Example: *You guys care about my grades, but being fit and healthy is just as important to my future. Please help me out. You won't regret it.*

_____

_____

_____

_____

_____

Pitch In

Offer to help out with shopping for healthier foods or cooking meals. If you can drive, offer to do the grocery shopping yourself (equipped with your family's list and your own).

Make It Simple

Sometimes parents are willing to help, but they're not sure how. You need to make it simple and easy for them to give you their support. That's where the list on pages 58–59 comes in. Go down the list and check off all the items you'd actually eat. Then give a copy to your parents. Now, when they hit the grocery store, they'll have a reference.

P.S. When picking items that need to be cooked, be sure either you or your parents are willing to do the honors. Otherwise, go for foods that can be thrown together sans the stove.

IF NOTHING WORKS…

Don't panic. It's possible your parents won't be supportive, no matter what you do. But you've still got options, and chances are not _everything_ in your pantry is disastrous for your diet. Scan your kitchen for the items I've listed on the next few pages (check off the ones you've got, if you think that'll help), and for Calorie Bargains. Then see if your parents will agree to at least keep the fattening foods out of sight.

Stocking the Diet-Savvy Kitchen

Proteins

- ❏ Albacore tuna (low-sodium, packed in water)
- ❏ Cottage cheese (fat-free)
- ❏ Eggs
- ❏ Nuts and seeds (low-sodium walnuts, almonds, and sunflower seeds)
- ❏ Peanut butter (try to get a 100% natural brand)
- ❏ Ricotta cheese (fat-free)
- ❏ Chicken breast
- ❏ Ground beef (extra-lean)
- ❏ Low-sodium turkey or chicken breast deli meat
- ❏ Sausage (turkey or chicken, low-fat)
- ❏ Shellfish
- ❏ Steak (extra-lean)
- ❏ Turkey breast
- ❏ White fish (like flounder, cod, halibut)

Vegetables (all vegetables are good)

- ❏ Artichokes
- ❏ Asparagus
- ❏ Beans (green, wax, snap)
- ❏ Beets
- ❏ Broccoli
- ❏ Brussels sprouts
- ❏ Cabbage (any type)
- ❏ Carrots
- ❏ Cauliflower

- ❏ Celery
- ❏ Cucumbers
- ❏ Eggplant
- ❏ Lettuce
- ❏ Mushrooms
- ❏ Onions
- ❏ Peppers (red, yellow, green)
- ❏ Radishes
- ❏ Salsa (fresh)
- ❏ Spinach
- ❏ Tomato
- ❏ Zucchini/Summer squash

Healthy Starches

- ❏ Beans
- ❏ Brown rice
- ❏ Oatmeal
- ❏ 100% whole-grain, high-fiber breads
- ❏ Whole-wheat pasta

Healthful Helpers

- ❏ Fat-free cooking spray
- ❏ Equal, Splenda sweeteners
- ❏ Herbal teas and seltzers
- ❏ Margarine spray (trans-fat-free)
- ❏ Mustard
- ❏ Salad dressings (low-cal, low-sugar, and low-sodium)
- ❏ Tomato juice
- ❏ Tomato sauce (low-fat, low-sodium)

The Kitchen Ditch-or-Hide List

Because they pack on pointless pounds, some foods just aren't worth having in the house, period. If your folks aren't willing to toss this stuff or delete it from their grocery list, that's understandable. Make a compromise by asking them to keep it somewhere out of sight—like in a specific drawer in the fridge or on an obscure shelf in the kitchen.

- ❏ Butter, or margarines with trans fats (check the label)
- ❏ Cake, cookie, brownie mixes
- ❏ Cakes
- ❏ Cheese (full-fat)
- ❏ Cookies
- ❏ Deli meats (full-fat)
- ❏ Ice cream
- ❏ Mayo
- ❏ Pizza
- ❏ Snack chips
- ❏ Soda
- ❏ Sugary cereals
- ❏ White breads
- ❏ White crackers
- ❏ White flour
- ❏ White rice

DINNER-IN-A-BOX

Want a hot meal that won't pack on the calories? Want it fast and easy? Stock up on frozen dinners. And make sure you pick options that are both healthy and filling. Here are a few great ones:

- **Healthy Choice Grilled Chicken Marinara** (10 oz.): 270 calories, 4.5g fat, 35g carbs, 5g fiber, 22g protein

- **Lean Cuisine's Chicken Chow Mein** (9 oz.): 230 calories, 3.5g fat, 35g carbs, 2g fiber, 14g protein

- **Michelina's Lean Gourmet Garden Bistro Asian Style** (9 oz.): 180 calories, 6g fat, 29g carbs, 5g fiber, 5g protein

- **Smart Ones Fajita Chicken Supreme** (9.25 oz.): 260 calories, 7g fat, 33g carbs, 3g fiber, 18g protein

- **Weight Watchers Smart Ones Fire-Grilled Chicken and Vegetables** (10 oz.): 280 calories, 3.5g fat, 45g carbs, 2g fiber, 18g protein

`DIET BONUS` Add some frozen vegetables or salad to the meal and cut up a piece of fruit for dessert.

`DIET BONUS` Put your frozen dinner on a real plate. It'll make it more satisfying.

Remember that if you need to eat two of these to be full, you aren't getting a Calorie Bargain. Only make the switch if it means you're eating *fewer* calories than you were before.

THE DIET-SAVVY STUDENT

How Diet-Savvy Is Your School?

Does your school make the grade when it comes to your diet? Circle the letter that fits.

1. Our snack machine is stocked with

   a. All healthy options, some of which are pretty tasty

   b. Mostly sweets and chips, with a scattering of healthy options

   c. Junk food only: candy bars, snack chips, and cookies

2. The cafeteria offers
    a. Low-cal, healthy options only
    b. Regular meals and healthier alternatives
    c. What you see is what you get—and what you get is pretty standard, fatty foods
3. The fresh fruits and vegetables in the cafeteria
    a. Are fresh and appetizing
    b. Are usually too spotty or nasty-looking to be taken seriously
    c. Must be invisible, because I only see overcooked veggies stewed in butter

Mostly A's: Top of the Food Chain

Wow. Unlike most schools, yours is top-notch when it comes to helping you get slim and healthy. You've got the setup to succeed, but go ahead and skim the following pages for extra hints.

Mostly B's: Somewhat Evolved

Your school may not be a trendsetter when it comes to creating a thinner, fitter generation, but it's starting to get with the program. Resisting temptation won't be easy, but at least you've got options. All of the tips below will be useful, and you can pay close attention to Pick to Win and Out of Sight, Out of Mind.

Mostly C's: A Diet Dinosaur

What cave did your cafeteria menu crawl out of? The poor selection of diet-friendly foods at your school may make you feel hopeless, and the overabundance of fattening options may be a challenge, but don't let it get to you. Keep reading for major help.

GET SQUARE WITH YOUR SCHOOL

Try these tactics to steer clear of weight-loss sabotage at school. Check off the ones you're willing to try.

Before You Go

Join the Breakfast Club

I know you've probably heard this before, but eating a good breakfast every morning is **critical** to losing weight and keeping it off.

According to the latest research, breakfast does all kinds of great things for you. It helps you live longer, and it improves your concentration. Most important, if you skip it, you're likely to starve all morning...and then you're very likely to overeat at lunch. And you know what that means.

> Research reported by the University of Colorado says that 78% of successful weight-loss maintainers eat breakfast every day of the week.

So what's a good breakfast? Well, you don't want to chow down on a high-calorie, high-fat morning meal. That would sort of defeat the purpose. Try healthy cereal and whole-wheat breads. They are usually lower in fat and higher in fiber than eggs and/or meats, and cereal is quick and easy to prepare. Just be sure the one you choose is low in sugar, and watch your portion size.

Diet Danger Zone
People who skip breakfast are 4.5 times more likely to be overweight. Yikes!

Just so you know, here's what works for me:

I eat six egg whites with broccoli and red peppers, and two pieces of 100% sugar-free whole-wheat toast with a no-cal margarine spray—a total of about 340 calories.

Get Packing

Don't knock packing lunch till you've tried it! Chances are that unless you have a stellar school cafeteria you can make tastier lunches than they can, anyway. Plus, packing your lunch gives you complete control. And control is a good thing, right?

SOME GREAT "BROWN BAG" LUNCHES

- 4-oz. white-meat turkey breast sandwich on 100% whole-wheat bread with one slice low-fat provolone, mustard, lettuce, tomato, onion: *360 calories*
- 1 Jell-O sugar-free, reduced-calorie pudding: *60 calories*
- 1 banana: *120 calories*
  Total calorie count: 540 calories

- 4 oz. smoked salmon on 100% whole-wheat bread with 2 tablespoons of low-fat cream cheese and dill: *390 calories*
- Low-fat Hickory Barbecue Kettle Chips (1-oz. bag): *110 calories*
- Nonfat, sugar-free vanilla yogurt: *90 calories*
  Total calorie count: *590 calories*

- 2 oz. hummus on 2 100% whole-wheat pitas with lettuce, tomato, and onion: *340 calories*
- 1 cup puffed Kashi: *70 calories*
- Progresso Vegetable Classics vegetable soup (1 cup): *80 calories*
- Apple: *80 calories*

  Total calorie count: *570 calories*

- 1 medium grilled chicken breast on 100% whole-wheat bread with roasted red peppers, lettuce, and mustard: *470 calories*
- 3-oz. side salad with a packet of Newman's Own low-fat balsamic vinaigrette: *55 calories*
- 1 orange: *60 calories*

  Total calorie count: *585 calories*

- 4 oz. (2 or 3 slices) deli ham on 100% whole-wheat bread with 1 slice low-fat Swiss cheese, lettuce, tomato, and mustard: *420 calories*
- ½ cup grapes: *60 calories*
- Campbell's Kitchen Classics chicken noodle soup (1 cup): *90 calories*

  Total calorie count: *570 calories*

Remove Temptation

- If you can't resist the snack machine at twelve, don't put money in your pocket at eight.
- If you're not packing your lunch, bring *only* the money you need to buy it, and no more.
- If you brought a snack to get you through midafternoon, keep it in your locker till it's time to munch.

Once You Get There

Pick to Win

At the cafeteria, avoid toppings such as gravy and butter or heavy salad dressing that will make your meal fattening. Fill up on fruits and vegetables if they've got them, as long as they're not smothered in butter or cheese.

Out of Sight, Out of Mind

If the snack machine's tempting, try an alternate route to class. If the smell of fries and pizza is drawing you away from the great lunch you packed, sit as far from the kitchen as possible.

SNACKS AND SIDES

Fruits and vegetables are low-cal, nutritious, filling, and don't have to be refrigerated or reheated. Apples, pears, grapes, and cut-up melon are durable and portable. Enjoy unsweetened all-natural applesauce packs or a small box of raisins. Other good choices:

- Nonfat yogurt is a great portable snack, but it's perishable, so pack it in an insulated bag or freeze it the night before.
- Low-calorie cereals (e.g., puffed Kashi at only 70 calories per cup) work well in a sealable bag. Choose cereals with no more than 160 calories per cup, and avoid added sugar and partially hydrogenated oil.
- Hard-boiled eggs pack well, and you can either eat only the whites or go for the entire egg for about 80 calories.
- Whole-grain rice cakes vary widely in calorie and fat content. Quaker lightly salted rice cakes are only 35 calories each.
- Energy bars tend to be high in calories and fat but are an okay alternative to candy bars. Don't exceed 200 calories.

- Soy chips or baked chips come packed in 1-ounce portions. Look for brands with fewer than 120 calories per ounce (potato chips are about 160).
- Jell-O sugar-free, reduced-calorie Pudding Snacks are 60 calories and can be kept in a cooler until lunch.
- Jell-O Smoothie Snacks are 100 calories and great if you're not a yogurt fan.
- Nabisco just came out with 100-calorie portion-controlled snack packs (e.g., Oreo Thin Crisps, Wheat Thins Minis) that have no trans fat. They're a decent snack once in a while, but don't start choosing them instead of fruit.

Remember Buddying Up?

Share lunch with your diet buddy. Try to impress each other with the delicious (and low-cal) foods you've brought. Enjoy the element of surprise.

DIET BONUS

"Be the change you wish to see in the world."
—*Mahatma Gandhi*

Are you the activist type? If your school's food choices are dismal, write a letter or circulate a petition outlining the excellent reasons for getting a better, healthier menu.

PACKING A SANDWICH? MAKE IT TASTY AND LOW-CAL

- Choose bread labeled "light" and 100% whole wheat—it's usually a 40- to 60-calorie savings over regular whole-wheat bread.
- Check out pita bread as an option—but it doesn't necessarily have fewer calories than bread. And watch out for bagels: They're low in fat but can contain up to 400 calories!
- Choose leaner cold cuts like turkey, chicken, roast beef, and ham. Avoid higher-fat meats like bacon, bologna, salami, pimiento loaf, and sausage.

- Be smart about peanut butter. It may have a lot of filling protein and "good" fat, but keep in mind that just 1 tablespoon also contains 95 calories.

- If you use cheese, go low- or no-fat. It's a great source of calcium and protein, but keep in mind that it still has calories.

- Skip sandwich salads with mayo—like tuna, chicken, or egg salads—unless you make them with light or fat-free mayonnaise. And avoid "club" sandwiches.

- For a creamy-textured topping with less fat, try a very thin slice of avocado. Other pretty harmless add-ons include mustard, ketchup, barbecue sauce, horseradish (not horseradish sauce), salsa, and balsamic vinegar. Or try a low-fat salad dressing.

SALAD SABOTAGE

Here are the calorie, fat, and carbohydrate counts for 3 tablespoons (a standard restaurant serving) of a few popular salad dressings.

- Blue cheese: 231 calories, 24g fat, 3g carbs
- Caesar: 233 calories, 25g fat, 2g carbs
- Ranch: 222 calories, 23g fat, 2g carbs
- Thousand Island: 177 calories, 17g fat, 2g carbs
- Creamy Italian: 150 calories, 15g fat, 3g carbs
- Olive oil and vinegar: 210 calories, 23g fat, 1g carbs

P.S. The tips above apply when you're hanging out at Blimpie's or Subway, too!

YOU: THE SOCIAL ANIMAL

You've got to have fun, right? And fun sometimes includes, well, eating with your friends. But don't make the mistake of nailing your diet at home and school, then blowing it all on the weekends. What would be the point of that?

Eating out is much less predictable than eating at home or at school, but it's just as easy to prepare for. It's actually pretty simple to guard against overindulging when you're socializing. And isn't *looking great* when you're doing it worth it?

FAST FOOD

If you've heard of or seen the movie *Supersize Me,* you probably have a healthy fear of fast food. The movie's creator goes on a McDonald's binge and ends up with huge amounts of extra weight, not to mention all sorts of health problems. Once you've seen it, it's hard to ever look at a Happy Meal happily again.

But let's face it, fast food is cheap, it tastes good, and it can be hard to avoid—especially when you're with your friends. So here's how to keep it together.

Look It Up: Use the Web sites on pages 74–75 to look up fast-foods Calorie Bargains and Calorie Rip-offs. Doing even a minute or two of research can pay off big-time. (You'll find that a McDonald's Quarter Pounder has 140 fewer calories than a Filet-O-Fish, for instance.)

Drink Up: Get water or skim milk instead of soda.

Stick to the Basics and Toss the Sauce: Say no to mayo, tartar sauce, and creamy dressings. Watch the nuts, croutons, and other salad add-ons. If you're getting a salad, go for low-calorie dressing, and don't drown the veggies. Give your sandwich a healthy, juicy taste by adding tomatoes instead of sauce. Look for grilled or broiled, not breaded or deep-fried. Order a salad or a broth-based soup as an appetizer.

Sub That Grub: Substitute mustard for mayo, a salad for a burger, fruit for the fries.

Beware of Portion Distortion: Treat yourself—to a thinner you, by resisting the urge to "supersize."

Remember to Blot a Lot: As I said back in the Calorie Bargains section, blotting your pizza, fries, and hamburger meat can save a lot of fat calories!

Don't Be Cheesy: Instead of cheese, opt for lettuce, tomato, and onion. Taking off just one slice of cheese will save you about 100 calories.

Veg Out: Top your pizza with vegetables instead of meat and cheese.

Dare to Share: Share a sandwich with a friend (and make it a healthy one).

Fast Food Lite

Here's a quick, at-a-glance list of lower-cal fast-food options at all your usual spots.

Arby's

- Chicken Club salad with light buttermilk ranch dressing: 250 calories, 7g fat, 28g carbs, 19g protein
- Regular roast beef sandwich: 320 calories, 13g fat, 34g carbs, 21g protein

FIT TIP Avoid the Market Fresh sandwiches (including turkey)—they all contain more than 700 calories.

Burger King

- Angus steak burger (low-carb): 260 calories, 18g fat, 2g carbs, 24g protein
- Chicken Whopper sandwich (on a small bun without mayo—ask for it): 320 calories, 7g fat, 31g carbs, 35g protein. Go "bare" and have just the chicken, no bun—it's only 150 calories.
- Fire-grilled shrimp garden salad: 200 calories, 10g fat, 12g carbs, 20g protein
- Veggie burger, no mayo: 300 calories, 7g fat, 46g carbs, 14g protein

FIT TIP Even the lowest-calorie dressing—the fat-free honey mustard—has 35 calories per ounce, which is high. Order anything low-carb and it comes without mayo, ketchup, or a bun, making it satisfying and low-cal.

Jack in the Box

- Asian chicken salad (no wonton strips) with low-fat balsamic dressing: 295 calories, 11.5g fat, 31g carbs, 17g protein
- Chicken fajita pita: 315 calories, 9g fat, 33g carbs, 22g protein
- Chicken sandwich (ask for low-fat herb mayo sauce instead of regular mayo), a side salad (hold the croutons), and low-fat balsamic dressing: 440 calories, 19.5g fat, 50g carbs, 18g protein

FIT TIP The specialty breads (e.g., Pannido or sourdough) have about 250 calories each—stick with a regular bun or go bunless!

KFC

- Caesar salad without dressing or croutons: 220 calories, 9g fat, 6g carbs, 29g protein
- Tender Roast sandwich: 390 calories, 19g fat, 24g carbs, 31g protein

FIT TIP Take the skin off the Original Recipe chicken breast to save a whopping 240 calories and 16g fat! And choose green beans (50 calories) or corn on the cob (150 calories) for a side.

McDonald's

- Caesar salad with grilled chicken (before dressing): 200 calories, 6g fat, 10g carbs, 28g protein
- California Cobb salad with grilled chicken (before dressing): 260 calories, 11g fat, 10g carbs, 32g protein
- Chicken McGrill sandwich without mayonnaise: 300 calories, 4.5g fat, 37g carbs, 27g protein

FIT TIP Always choose grilled rather than crispy chicken, and hold the mayo. Newman's Own low-fat balsamic vinaigrette is the best dressing at 40 calories for 2 ounces, compared with 120 calories for Cobb dressing or a whopping 190 calories for Caesar.

Subway

- Roasted chicken noodle soup (1 cup): 60 calories, 1.5g fat, 7g carbs, 6g protein
- Savory turkey breast sandwich (6-inch): 280 calories, 4.5g fat, 46g carbs, 18g protein

- Veggie Delite sandwich (6-inch): 230 calories, 3g fat, 44g carbs, 9g protein

FIT TIP If you're really hungry, ask for a double-meat 6-inch sub: roast beef (360 calories), turkey (340 calories), or ham (380 calories).

Taco Bell

- Fresco Burrito Supreme (chicken): 350 calories, 8g fat, 50g carbs, 19g protein
- Fresco-Style Chicken Ranchero tacos (2): 340 calories, 8g fat, 40g carbs, 24g protein

FIT TIP Order everything "Fresco Style"—meaning with salsa and without cheese or sauce.

Wendy's

- Mandarin chicken salad with almonds (no noodles) and fat-free French dressing: 400 calories, 14g fat, 40g carbs, 27g protein. You can also have the salad without the almonds and save another 130 calories.
- Quarter-pound Classical Singles (2) with no buns and nothing on them except ketchup: 415 calories, 26g fat, 4g carbs, 38g protein
- Ultimate Chicken Grill sandwich: 360 calories, 7g fat, 44g carbs, 31g protein

FIT TIP Even the "reduced-calorie" dressings at Wendy's are a bit higher than those at other fast-food restaurants—use sparingly.

NET SAVINGS

You can get all the info you need to make your own fast-food Calorie Bargains online. Go to the URLs below for stuff like the calorie counts and fat content of your favorite fast foods. Trust me, coming up with a few trade-offs ahead of time will make it easy to go the automatic route when you hit McDonald's or Chick-fil-A with your pals.

Arby's: http://www.arbys.com/nutrition/arbys_us_nutrition.pdf

Blimpie: http://blimpie.com/nutritional_analyzer/nutritional.php

Boston Market: http://www.bostonmarket.com/food/index.jsp?page=nutrition

Burger King: http://www.burgerking.com/food/nutrition/nutritionwizard/index.aspx

Carl's Jr.: http://www.carlsjr.com/nutrition/index.html

Chick-fil-A: http://chick-fil-a.com/menucalculator.asp

Domino's Pizza: http://www.dominos.com/c1256b42005511e1/repositoryfile/nutrition_pdf/$file/nutritionalguidelines.pdf

Hardee's: http://www.hardees.com/nutrition/

Jack in the Box: http://www.jackinthebox.com/ourfood/build.php

KFC: http://www.kfc.com/kitchen/nutrition.htm

Long John Silver's: http://www.ljsilvers.com/nutrition/default.htm

McDonald's: http://www.mcdonalds.com/usa/eat/nutrition_info.html

Papa Gino's: http://www.papaginos.com/nutrition.html

Papa John's: http://papajohns.com/menu/index.htm

Pizza Hut: http://www.pizzahut.com/menu/nutritioninfo.asp

Round Table Pizza: http://www.roundtablepizza.com/rtp/hi/

Sbarro: http://www.sbarro.com/menu/nutrition_chart.cfm

Schlotzsky's: http://www.schlotzskys.com/downloads/nutrition.pdf

Subway: http://www.subway.com/applications/nutritioninfo/index.aspx

Taco Bell: http://www.yum.com/nutrition/documents/tb_nutrition.pdf

Wendy's: http://www.wendys.com/food/index.jsp?country=us&lang=en

Whataburger: http://www.whataburger.com/menulist.cfm

White Castle: http://www.whitecastle.com/_pages/nutrition.asp

"IN"CONVENIENCE STORES

A lot of times when you're in a rush, you end up at quickie stores like 7-Eleven, Circle K, and Wawa, or other so-called convenience stores loaded with high-calorie snacks. Check out the comparisons below of some common convenience store finds, so next time you're stuck, you'll know which foods are Calorie Bargains—and which are Calorie Rip-offs. Also, don't forget that many convenience stores have started carrying fruit, which is pretty much always the smarter choice. For example, 7-Eleven has fresh fruit cups—some just with grapes, some assorted. And it seems like there's always an orange or an apple in most of these stores. A few even have hard-boiled eggs, a good option!

7-Eleven Slurpee or Big Gulp vs. 1 Pint of Häagen-Dazs Chocolate Ice Cream

Of course the ice cream has more calories, but the difference is smaller than you might think. A Coca-Cola Classic Super Big Gulp (44 ounces) has 660 calories and 176 grams of carbs. By comparison, a pint of Häagen-Dazs chocolate ice cream has 1,080 calories.

FIT TIP If you want the ice cream, go for the Häagen-Dazs Vanilla & Almonds bar—320 calories, 12 grams of fat, and 22 grams of carbs—instead of the entire pint. Otherwise, try a 12-ounce Crystal Light Raspberry (or Lemon-Lime) Ice Slurpee for just 50 calories, or a 22-ounce of the same flavors for 90 calories. Best choice of all? The Diet Pepsi Slurpee—it's virtually calorie-free!

Potato Chips vs. Terra Chips vs. Doritos vs. Peanut Butter Sandwich Crackers

All the chips (yes, even the Terra Chips) are pretty much the same, but the stores I visited stocked only 2-ounce bags of Doritos and Wise chips (most chip bags are 1 ounce). In that case, the peanut butter crackers are your best bet—at least you're getting some good nutrients.

Terra Chips (1 oz.): 140 calories, 7g fat, 18g carbs

Wise potato chips (1 oz.): 150 calories, 10g fat, 14g carbs

Frito Lay peanut butter sandwich crackers (1 package):
   210 calories, 10g fat, 23g carbs

Ready Pac Chicken Caesar Salad with Dressing vs. Mediterranean-style Turkey Sandwich vs. ham-and-cheese Hot Pocket

Be careful—the salad package says only 230 calories, but it *also* says it contains two servings. Yeah, right! The total is 460 calories, 42 grams of fat, 8 grams of carbs, and 1,220 milligrams of sodium. And what about the turkey? Remember, these are prepackaged sandwiches, so you can't ask anyone to hold the mayo or the high-calorie special sauces. In this particular case, the turkey is still the winner at only 400 calories, but always check the label. And as for the ham-and-cheese Hot Pocket, it has 540 calories, 18 grams of fat, 74 grams of carbs, and 1,410 milligrams of sodium.

FIT TIP Sauces are loaded with calories, so scrape off any excess. (Just 1 tablespoon of mayo—the typical base for many sandwich sauces—has 100 calories.) Look for low-calorie soup as a different option—many times, all you have to do is heat it up or add hot water.

Sausage, Egg, and Cheese on English Muffin vs. Coffee and a Banana Walnut Muffin

The banana muffin may sound safe, but it's quite "expensive" at 605 calories, 30 grams of fat, and 72 grams of carbs. The breakfast combo is a much better deal at 450 calories, 24 grams of fat, and 37 grams of carbs.

FIT TIP Go for small packs of cereal (90 to 150 calories), and use skim milk. Also, if you're set on an egg sandwich or burrito, choose either sausage *or* ham, or cheese—not both meat *and* cheese. And you can always remove one of the links or take off some of the cheese before you heat it up.

7-Eleven Quarter-pound Big Bite Hot Dog vs. Don Miguel Beef Steak Burrito

A close call—the hot dog alone carries 365 calories, 34 grams of fat, 2 grams of carbs, and a whopping 1,137 milligrams of sodium. Add the 120-calorie bun and you've got a 485-calorie snack. The 7-ounce burrito is a better choice, with 390 calories, 8 grams of fat, 61 grams of carbs and 930 milligrams of sodium.

FIT TIP Go smaller with the 2-ounce Big Bite hot dog—just 280 calories, including the bun—and avoid calorie-laden condiments such as cheese and chili. Stick to the 5- to 7-ounce burritos, and steer clear of the 10-ounce burrito, which has close to 700 calories!

Nutri-Grain Bar vs. PowerBar vs. Clif Bar vs. Snickers

Remember, size matters. The Nutri-Grain is lowest in calories and is your best best, but it's also about one-third the size of the others here, so make sure eating just one will satisfy you, or you'll end up doubling up and losing the calorie benefit. Here's the breakdown:

Nutri-Grain bar: 140 calories, 3g fat, 27g carbs (contains high-fructose corn syrup and trans fat)

Chocolate PowerBar: 230 calories, 2g fat, 45g carbs (contains high-fructose corn syrup)

Chocolate Brownie Clif Bar: 240 calories, 4.5g fat, 45g carbs (organic and contains no trans fat)

Snickers bar: 280 calories, 14g fat, 35g carbs (contains sugar and saturated and trans fat)

FIT TIP Probably the hardest part of leaving a convenience store without buying anything unhealthy is staring at the candy bars while you're waiting in line. Stay focused and avoid impulse buys.

Arizona Iced Tea with Ginseng vs. Gatorade vs. Orange Juice

A 20-ounce bottle of Arizona iced tea has 175 calories and 45 grams of carbs, definitely a better bet caloriewise than Tropicana Pure Premium Original orange juice. Sixteen ounces of the orange juice packs 220 calories and 52 grams of carbs. Of course, it's also got 900 milligrams of potassium and tons of vitamin C. The ultimate winner for low-cal here is Gatorade Lemon-Lime sports drink, with 50 calories and 14 grams of carbs per 8 ounces.

FIT TIP Try no-calorie flavored coffee, like 7-Eleven's chocolate-cherry coffee, and use skim milk.

RESTAURANTS

Eating out at sit-down restaurants has its high points, and one of them is that it can seem like a less greasy alternative to fast food. But that's only true if you do it right. Here's how.

Get Your Input In Early: When choosing a place to eat, there's no harm in letting your friends know you'd rather stay away from buffets, all-you-can-eat restaurants, or other places you know are diet minefields. Let them know you're not just being a pain in the butt by suggesting several other places you could go.

Do I Really Want to Eat That? For lots of people, devouring the bread basket is a way to fill time, not just their stomachs, until the real meal comes. If your friends agree, ask the waitperson not to bring bread to the table. Or, if you've got to have a slice, at least don't smother it with butter or dip it in olive oil.

P.S. Don't feel forced to order an appetizer just because everyone else is.

Eat Before: Have a high-fiber snack before you go out, like an apple or even a bowl of cereal. And don't skip meals just to "save up" for a night out. The hungrier you are when you're out, the more you will eat.

P.S. Drink lots of water with your meal—it'll help to fill you up. So will ordering a salad or a broth-based soup as an appetizer.

Monster-size Portions Ahead! Lots of restaurants make their servings larger than any human being needs. Consider splitting a dish with a friend or having half the meal wrapped up ahead of time to take home. You might even skip to the Healthy Options section of the menu to avoid temptation.

Skip the Pasta and the Fries:

French fries (1 medium order): *450 calories*

Pasta with meat sauce (1 cup): *301 calories*

Enough said.

Customize: Don't be afraid or embarrassed to ask if you can get something broiled instead of fried, get sauce or sour cream or dressing on the side, or get your meal without the gloppy cheese topping. It takes two seconds and can save countless calories.

GO OUT, EAT SKINNY

At-a-glance list of lower-cal options at your favorite restaurants.

CARIBBEAN AND AFRICAN

Look for: Poached, steamed, or grilled dishes; stews, curries (without coconut or coconut milk)

Look out for: Fried foods; coconut, peanuts, cream, puddings, fritters

Best bet: Broiled fillet red snapper, or jerk chicken without sauce

CHINESE

Look for: Stir-fried, simmered, steamed, or roasted foods; bean curd (not fried), lobster sauce, tomato sauce, light sauce, oyster sauce, brown rice

Look out for: Fried, crispy, or breaded foods; eggs, peanuts or cashews, hoisin sauce, fruit, sweet-and-sour sauce, soy or teriyaki sauce (high in sodium)

Best bet: Steamed chicken, fish, or tofu with vegetables, sauce on the side

INDIAN, THAI, OR VIETNAMESE

Look for: Stir-fried, steamed, or simmered foods; soup (without coconut milk), kebabs, biryani (without nuts), curried vegetables

Look out for: Crispy or fried items; coconut, cream

Best bet: Tandori or tikka (grilled, skewered Indian dish), or any steamed fish with vegetables

ITALIAN

Look for: Marinara, primavera, or arrabiata sauces; roasted, grilled, or steamed foods; thin-crust pizza, pasta, tomatoes

Look out for: Foods that are fried, stuffed, or prepared parmigiana-style; Alfredo, white, or carbonara sauces; cheese

Best bet: Pasta with tomato-based sauce; chicken or fish prepared without oil

JAPANESE

Look for: Broiled, grilled, or steamed items; sushi, sashimi, soup, hijiki, oshitashi

Look out for: Fried or battered foods; soy, teriyaki, or tamari sauces (high in sodium); tempura, duck, cream cheese or mayo (in sushi), eel, fish roe

Best bets: Vegetable or fish sushi rolls (not fried) or tuna nigiri

MEXICAN

Look for: Grilled items (like fajitas); simmered, shredded, or minced items; soft tortillas/soft tacos, beans, enchilada sauce, salsa

Look out for: Deep-fried foods; tacos, taco salad, cheese, chips, guacamole, nachos, huevos, sour cream, bunuelos

Best bet: Char-grilled chicken burrito or fajita (dry/no oil) with salsa, no cheese

STEAKHOUSE

Look for: Grilled or baked foods or meats prepared au jus; sirloin, filet, chicken, shrimp

Look out for: Battered or fried foods; béarnaise or hollandaise sauces; New York strip, T-bone, porterhouse, or rib-eye steaks; prime rib, onion rings

Best bet: Filet mignon prepared without oil with small baked potato and salad on the side

Chain Restaurants

You probably eat at some of these restaurants once in a while, with your friends or your family. The easy thing about eating at a chain restaurant is that their menus are mostly the same everywhere, so you can walk in the door knowing what to order and what to cross off your list. Here are some Calorie Bargains at eight of the biggest national chain restaurants, and some extra tips for eating "better" at all of them.

* All calorie counts marked with asterisks are estimates from a registered dietician, formerly published in "The Diet Detective" column.

Applebee's

- Onion soup au gratin: 150 calories, 8g fat
- Grilled shrimp skewer salad: 210 calories, 2g fat
- Teriyaki shrimp skewers with rice pilaf and vegetables: 290 calories, 2g fat
- Grilled tilapia with mango salsa and steamed vegetables: 320 calories, 6g fat
- Mesquite chicken salad: 250 calories, 4g fat

FIT TIP Applebee's has teamed up with Weight Watchers to create some excellent low-calorie dishes. The portion sizes are the same as regular meals, because it's the ingredients themselves that are healthier. Steer clear of the bleu cheese sirloin, which is likely to be well over 1,200 calories. Don't be fooled by the sandwiches and roll-ups; they're high in calories, too, especially with fries, cheese, and sauces. Avoid all the Neighborhood Favorites. If you really want dessert, you can probably fit in the chocolate raspberry layer cake (230 calories, 3 grams fat).

Chili's

- Guiltless chicken platter with rice, corn on the cob, and steamed vegetables: 580 calories, 9g fat, 85g carbs
- Guiltless Grill salmon with steamed fresh veggies and black beans: 480 calories, 14g fat, 31g carbs
- Guiltless tomato basil pasta: Skip the cheese to bring the total down to 650 calories, 14g fat, 107g carbs.

FIT TIP This chain's Guiltless Grill menu offers great low-calorie choices like the ones above. And Chili's will make adjustments to all of its dishes because they're made to order. Most of the appetizers are dangerous bets, though, especially the Awesome Blossom. Avoid the fajitas at more than 1,000 calories—the meat and vegetables are cooked with loads of oil, and the toppings can almost double the calorie count. Choose low-cal salad dressings, such as fat-free honey-mustard or low-fat ranch.

Olive Garden

- Minestrone soup: 164 calories, 1g fat
- Linguine alla marinara: 551 calories, 8g fat
- Capellini pomodoro: 644 calories, 14g fat
- Chicken giardino (ask for whole-wheat pasta): 560 calories, 15g fat
- Pork Filettino with grilled vegetables: 340 calories, 9g fat (does not include demi-glaze or marinade)*
- Salmon piccata with vegetables: 440 calories, 21g fat*

FIT TIP Stick with Garden Fare choices, designated with an olive branch. Also, shave calories by ordering lunch portions. And order low-fat Italian dressing (37 calories per serving) or low-fat parmesan peppercorn dressing (45 calories per serving) for any salad. Assume that the non–Garden Fare items have more than 1,000 calories, especially the creamy, fried, and cheesy dishes. Finally, watch out for those bread sticks. At 140 calories apiece, they can make any meal a diet disaster.

Outback Steakhouse

- Shrimp, chicken, or steak Griller: Request no butter or glaze, and skip the pineapple. Get a baked potato with ketchup or salsa (no butter or sour cream) instead of rice. With the house salad, hold the croutons and cheese and sprinkle it with low-fat dressing, such as fat-free Tangy Tomato, fresh lemon juice, or red wine vinegar and olive oil. 625, 715, and 775 calories, respectively.*

- Chicken on the Barbie: Order it without butter. Again, order a baked or sweet potato and a house salad. 640 calories*

- Grilled shrimp on the Barbie: Order with cocktail or barbecue sauce and no butter. 275 calories*

FIT TIP Almost everything—including the steamed vegetables—is cooked with butter or a fattening sauce. Get used to saying, "No butter, please!" For steak, your best bet is filet mignon (about 450 calories). Avoid Aussie cheese fries, which are loaded with more than 2,000 calories!

P.F. Chang's

- Seared ahi tuna: 220 calories, 5g fat, 18g carbs
- Shrimp dumplings (steamed): 320 calories, 12g fat, 26g carbs

- Shrimp with lobster sauce (dinner portion): 560 calories, 27g fat, 22g carbs
- Cantonese shrimp: 380 calories, 15g fat, 17g carbs
- Wonton soup (1 cup): 52 calories, 3g fat, 4g carbs

FIT TIP This is probably the only Chinese restaurant in the country that publishes all of its nutrition info on its Web site, so check it out for a full report on calorie deals and steals. Try making a meal out of appetizers and sides, like the seared ahi tuna, Sichuan asparagus, or Shanghai cucumbers. Avoid most salads—the Oriental chicken salad, for instance, has 940 calories. Steer clear of the spare ribs (1,410 calories) and anything kung pao, like kung pao chicken (1,230 calories).

Red Lobster

- Live Maine lobster (1¼ pound) with a baked potato topped with pico de gallo and a garden salad with red wine vinaigrette: 431 calories, 8g fat, 53g carbs
- Jumbo shrimp cocktail dinner with seasoned broccoli and wild rice pilaf: 511 calories, 8g fat, 50g carbs
- King crab legs: 490 calories, 9g fat, 0g carbs

FIT TIP The LightHouse menu makes it easier to choose wisely here. Also, you can get the tilapia, rainbow trout, or salmon in full or half orders, so you can save calories on portion size. Substitute cocktail sauce whenever a dish comes with a side of butter—it saves 115 calories per serving. And pico de gallo on your potato adds only 6 calories, which definitely beats butter! Avoid the shrimp lover's combo, which basically fries up healthy food and makes it unhealthy. Watch out for the salads, too—they have high-calorie dressings, cheese, and other unhealthy goodies.

Ruby Tuesday

- Salad Bar Extravaganza: Avoid the high-calorie dressings, nuts, and croutons. Go for the light ranch dressing at 55 calories per ounce.

- Smart Eating petite sirloin: 222 calories, 8g fat

- Smart Eating onion soup (NOT French onion): 198 calories, 13g fat

- Asian steamed dumplings (appetizer): 486 calories, 21g fat. Split this with someone or have it as a meal; there are six dumplings.

- Smart Eating turkey burger wrap with a side of creamy mashed cauliflower: 574 calories, 28g fat

FIT TIP Check out their Smart Eating menu for extra good choices. Avoid the Buffalo wings at 912 calories. The salads are also high in calories—the Carolina chicken salad has 847 calories. Many of the "low-carb" items are high in calories. Avoid the cheesy spinach dip and all the platters.

T.G.I. Friday's

- Barbecue Jack chicken with black beans and corn salsa, herbed rice, grilled vegetables, and steamed broccoli: 500 calories, 10g fat

- Jack Daniel's salmon: Skip the mashed potatoes (try baked instead). Also, request no oil or butter on your salmon. 615 calories*

- Santa Fe chicken salad: Get the Chipotle Ranch dressing on the side. 500 calories, 10g fat

- Bruschetta grouper with steamed herbed rice and broccoli: Request the balsamic glaze on the side. 500 calories, 10g fat

FIT TIP Almost all the other options on the menu—including appetizers, Atkins menu items, and salads (which may be over 700 calories with dressing)—are high in calories. Ask for your dish to be prepared grilled or broiled and with little or no cheese or sauce.

PARTIES

Parties can be another danger zone for your diet. Here's how to protect yourself without spoiling all the fun:

Lend a Hand (or a Snack): Offer to bring snacks (nonfattening ones, naturally) or to help make the food once you get there.

WHAT YOU JUST GOT

In this step, you learned how to take control of your surroundings instead of letting your surroundings control you. And now you've also got the know-how to get the support that will make it last.

NEXT UP

You know how to protect your diet from unhealthy surroundings and the wrong kinds of food choices, but what about from your own worst enemy—you? Move on to Step 4 for a deeper look at how what's in your head and your heart can turn a good diet bad...and how to turn it around.

STEP 4 Be a "Diet Detective": Discover Your "Fat" Pattern

MAKING IT STICK

You've probably learned from personal experience that *knowing* how to eat for a better body and actually *doing* it are two very different things. And that's true for just about everyone.

There's a good reason for this. And luckily, there's an even better way to fix it.

The next two steps are going to show you how.

CAUTION: YOUR PAST CAN BURN YOU!

Let's say you walked into the kitchen one day and touched a hot pot on the stove. And let's say the pot was so scalding that it burned your hand. You'd think twice before making the same mistake again, wouldn't you?

Trying + Failing = Learning

When something "burns" us—like a mistake we made, a choice that didn't yield great results, or a theory that turned out to be dead wrong—it gives us an opportunity to change our behavior. Bad experiences can be our best teachers.

So why do we make the same dieting mistakes over and over? Especially when we've been burned so many times?

One reason is *patterns*, or *habits*. Patterns aren't always as clear-cut as the one established by burning ourselves on a hot stove. And most of them aren't nearly as obvious. If you tackle boredom by chowing down on chips, that's a pattern. Or if your parents used sugary snacks to comfort you when you were little and now you use them to comfort *yourself,* that's a pattern, too.

But patterns aren't always bad for you. For instance, you might always go for a walk after dinner or always eat a healthy breakfast.

And patterns aren't just about food, either. You use them to deal with every part of your life—your friendships, your parents, your schoolwork—*everything*. And as long as they're not hurting you, patterns are fine. In this book we are trying to break the negative patterns and start new, more positive patterns.

BUT WAIT, THERE'S HOPE!

I said changing patterns wasn't easy, but it *is* totally doable… *if* you have the right equipment. That's true even if you've failed time and time again.

➔ In fact, the more you try to lose weight and fail, the greater chance you have of succeeding the next time.

Okay, I know what you're thinking: "If failing is the key to losing weight, I should weigh about two pounds right now." But it's not that simple. All I'm saying is, past efforts count— no matter what the outcome. The key is *doing something* with the experience you've got so you can *break the pattern.*

It basically boils down to this: **You are the creator of all your own attitudes about food.** Which means you are in the unique and powerful position of being able to change them.

Step 4 is going to show you how to do it. You've been burned for the last time.

BECOME A "DIET DETECTIVE"

In this step, you're going to become a "diet detective" and search out clues about your diet patterns. What's been holding you back from losing weight? What's been keeping you from sticking to your diet promises? What, if anything, has actually worked—at least a little? Once you understand what you've been doing wrong and why you've been doing it, you'll be able to change it. **By looking at the past, you'll be able to make changes that will help rewrite your future**. In case you don't know what future I'm talking about, it's the one where getting and keeping a body you're thrilled with is easy, automatic, and forever.

BRAIN FOOD

Eating isn't just about survival. It's also connected to our minds and hearts. We often use food to soothe ourselves when we're sad, entertain ourselves when we're bored, distract us from our stress, give us something to do with our hands and mouths when we're nervous.

Think of some things you use food for, other than filling your stomach. I'll bet you've got at least a couple.

Example: *Eating cheers me up when I'm depressed.*

Any eating pattern you have—whether it's craving candy after meals, snacking late at night, mindless eating in front of the TV—provides you with some kind of emotional and/or physical benefit. That's why you adopted the pattern in the first place. It's important to remember this, because as we delve into your past and learn a bit more about you, it will help you to remember that you shouldn't be hard on yourself for being the way you are. **There's a reason for everything you do.** And it's not lack of willpower. It's because you've benefited from your diet patterns at some time, in some way. Even if your body and your self-esteem haven't.

While eating has given you benefits like comfort or entertainment, those benefits have been at a huge cost. And I'm guessing you're no longer willing to pay that price. By uncovering the bad patterns and coming up with good, satisfying, and simple ways to replace them, you won't have to.

FIND YOUR NEGATIVE DIET PATTERNS

Let's look for clues about your past dieting patterns.

In your dieting past, did you vow to exercise three times a week and then get "too busy" to do it? Did you try to go low-carb and find it made chips more irresistible than ever? Did you vow to cook your own healthy dinner every night and then get tired of the work that went into it?

It's not easy to look at our past mistakes. I know taking an honest look at your history takes a lot of bravery. But trust me, it will pay off by giving you a better future.

On the following page, I want you to tell the truth about diet strategies you've used, what didn't work and why, and then I want you to look for the pattern. For instance, maybe you got sick of an exercise routine (you need variety); maybe you tried to restrict yourself too much and you couldn't stick to it (you need freedom); maybe you didn't like cooking enough to do it every night (you need to simplify your meals)—whatever!

Last but not least, think hard about what you can learn from the experience before you fill in the last column. There are no right or wrong answers, but it's a great opportunity to brainstorm about what you can do better next time.

A diet strategy that didn't work	Why it didn't work	Looking for patterns	What I've learned
I tried to eat the same low-fat breakfast every day.	I got bored and started adding sugary cereals to liven things up.	When I try to eat the same food every day, I cave.	I need variety. Which means I need to come up with a variety of low-fat breakfast options to choose from.

A diet strategy that didn't work	Why it didn't work	Looking for patterns	What I've learned
I promised myself I'd go for a walk every morning. I would set my alarm clock, my TV, and the alarm on the phone, but I could never drag myself out of bed.	I hate exercising in the morning.	I do all my best work in the afternoon.	I'm just not a morning person. If I really wanted to exercise, I should have done it after school or after dinner.

FIND YOUR DIET SUCCESS PATTERNS

Chances are not all of your diet tactics have failed. Even if the diet itself didn't rock you with earth-shattering results, there were probably a few small strategies—big or small—that actually worked. If these are a little harder to come up with than your diet failures, it's hardly surprising! But give it a try, anyway—if you can't come up with five, do as many as you can.

THINGS YOU MAY HAVE LEARNED FROM...

Atkins: "I don't need two slices of bread to feel satisfied with a sandwich—just the meat and veggies, wrapped in a lettuce leaf."

South Beach: "Now I know the difference between good carbs and bad carbs."

Weight Watchers: "Surrounding myself with supportive people keeps me motivated."

Jenny Craig: "Portion control (like frozen meals) really works for me."

A diet strategy that worked	Why it worked	Looking for patterns	What I've learned
I kept a stockpile of hard-boiled eggs in the fridge.	I love eggs and I could just grab one out of the fridge, remove the fatty yolk part, and make it part of my meal.	If something's tasty and easy to stockpile, I'll stick with it.	I need to come up with other food options that I like, that I can easily prepare ahead of time and grab when the time is right.

A diet strategy that worked	Why it worked	Looking for patterns	What I've learned
I started keeping a food diary and wrote down all my meals.	I could see every single thing I ate and figure out the calories and fat in all of it.	When I'm not paying attention, I eat way more calories and fat than I think I do.	It seemed kind of pointless at first, but it turned out to be really helpful. I realized I could replace a lot of what I was eating with lower-calorie stuff.

OKAY, NOW WHAT?

So, now take all the things you've written down and go through them carefully. What you do next is simple: Just remember what worked and what didn't so that you can *use* the *good* stuff and try *not to repeat the bad.*

Does "not repeating the bad" sound a little easier said than done? That's because we're only *partly* finished with our detective work. Keep going!

Trust me, as you move forward, it'll all come together.

> **Think Positive**
>
> When replacing your patterns, don't say things like "I need to stop eating junk food" or "I will never watch television again." Go with positive statements, such as "I'm going to start eating no-fat frozen yogurt instead of ice cream."

YOUR DIET STYLE

You have your own style of dressing and walking and talking, so why not your own style of dieting? The ways people approach diets may differ, but they can be summed up in seven major types. Take this quiz to find out which one (or two, or more) you've got.

What's Your Diet Style?

Circle the letter that *best* describes you:

1. You usually tackle a diet by
   a. Looking for foods with eye-grabbing labels like "low-fat," "diet," or "low-carb," then stocking up
   b. Adopting the most up-to-date diet out there. If it's new, it's probably better
   c. Waiting for the right time. You don't want to start before you're ready

d Eating anything you want and then exercising to compensate. There's no point depriving yourself when you can just work it off

e. Forgetting it. You're just too overwhelmed to concentrate on a diet

f. Making promises, but then finding so many reasons to break them—like a bake sale at school or a bad day at school

g. Cutting out as much food as you can and sticking to a strict set of rules that you break, temporarily, when the deprivation is just too much

2. Your diet motto is

   a. "Anything labeled 'diet' is fair game"

   b. "The latest is the greatest"

   c. "The sun'll come out tomorrow"

   d. "Eat now, run it off later"

   e. "I'll try to fit it into my schedule"

   f. "I'm fine with cutting down, but I need to 'treat' myself"

   g. "The more foods I cut, the better. I can always take little breaks"

3. On your diet, you'd be lost without

   a. Labels to show you the way

   b. The next trend

   c. Knowing you could start tomorrow

   d. Exercise

   e. The to-do list in your planner…where exercise is marked #25

   f. Sometimes being able to reward yourself with food

   g. The option to take time-outs from your strict routine

Like I said, maybe two of the descriptions below apply to you—maybe even three or four. It can't hurt to read as many as you think might apply. And if you don't see yourself in any of the descriptions—give it some thought. What kind of diet style do you think *you* have?

Mostly A's: The Diet Label Lover

As long as something's labeled "diet," "low-carb," or "low-fat," you assume it's fair game. The problem is that low-fat foods are typically high in sugar, and low-sugar or low-carb foods are usually high in fat. Forget about letting those deceptive labels tell you what works. By using what you've learned about reading nutrition labels, you'll be able to use those foods without letting them ruin your diet.

Mostly B's: The Diet Groupie

Hallelujah! You tackle every new diet as if it were the next great religion. You buy the books, follow the rules, and stay on the lookout for the BBD—the Bigger, Better Diet. Too bad that miracle they're promising you never arrives! Why focus all that energy on waiting for a BBD when you can use your ready-made Calorie Bargains to make your diet automatic—and *really end your weight woes forever.*

Mostly C's: The Procrastinator

Hey, procrastinator, how many times have you said you were going to start your diet after the weekend, after the holidays, at the end of the school year? No matter what the excuse, putting off the happier, thinner you doesn't help. If you want to lose weight, you can start *anytime.* And the sooner you start, the sooner you'll see the pounds slip away!

Mostly D's: The Unreal Exercise Junkie

As an unreal exercise junkie, you think that exercise can solve all your weight problems—and when it doesn't deliver, you probably see it as final proof that fat's in your genes and there's nothing you can do about it.

The fact is, exercising does give you a *huge* advantage. But if your eating habits don't change, too, it's not going to get you very far. Try making Calorie Bargains and *eating* for a thinner you, too.

Mostly E's: The Just-Too-Busy Body

Your life is hectic! You've got so much on your plate—school, homework, social life, family life—that you don't have time to try to eat better. But hey, the truth is that eating healthy doesn't take *any more time* than not eating healthy. What you need are quick strategies (even a list) for quicker meals and snacks that are low in calories but tasty and filling. Keep your list of instant Calorie Bargains handy. And keep going!

Mostly F's: The Justifier

You probably have great reasons for your eating habits. Maybe you overeat at home because your life there is the pits. Maybe eating provides a "treat" when you're feeling low. But using food as a bandage or a reward is doing you more harm than good. You need to understand that while you may not be responsible for the stuff that makes you want to eat, you *are* responsible for how you choose to deal with it. It's up to you to solve your weight problem and live life, not hide from it. Keep reading.

Mostly G's: The Restrictor

You tend to go on diets that cut out all sorts of foods—bread, vegetables, fruits, no carbs, all carbs, no fat—whatever! You follow these diets to the letter for as long as you can, but you're starved at mealtimes, or you get restless after a couple of weeks, *and then* you resort to devouring whatever is in front of you...and a lot of it! You may have entire days where you "take a break."

Listen, your diet deprivation is making you *miserable*—and it isn't helping you shed the pounds. So why keep it up? You need to build a diet that doesn't make you feel deprived, so you won't want to binge. The kind like you're building with the help of this book.

WHAT YOU JUST GOT

Way to go! If you tackled this step full-throttle, it took a lot of courage, because facing your own negative patterns is one of the hardest things you can do, period. But thanks to your efforts, you've discovered some important clues about your own worst habits (and some good habits, too)—and you've started to think about how to use these clues to turn your weight-loss efforts into permanent success.

NEXT UP

It's not over yet! You're still on the "pattern" clue trail, and it's about to lead you to the diet traps that can get in the way of your weight loss. You'll be surprised at how these traps can derail a diet—and how easy they are to manage once you know how to spot them.

STEP 5 Escape the Diet Traps

Many of us eat without really *noticing* what we're eating or even that we're eating at all—in front of the TV or slumped over a textbook to study. We're religious about mealtimes but make up for it with little eating splurges to "get us through the rough spots." We take little "diet vacations" when there are events or occasions that seem to call for them. We have little talks with ourselves that go something like this: "I'd hate to let this opportunity to enjoy some birthday cake/an ice-cream sundae/some apple pie/some cookies pass me by. You only live once."

Meanwhile, these habits are causing life to pass us by instead.

IF YOU ONLY LIVE ONCE, WHY STAY TRAPPED?

You've already discovered some of your diet patterns, and that's going to pay off. But facing the past is only half the pattern picture—you've also got to know what pitfalls are waiting for you from here on out. I promise, they won't be a threat once you know how to face them.

WHAT ARE DIET TRAPS?

Diet traps come in many forms, such as:

- A certain food you can't resist
- A situation that makes you want to eat for comfort
- A celebration that revolves around food.

Diet traps sabotage your diet. They weaken your determination to lose weight and make it hard to stick to a routine, even if that routine is totally working for you. Even when everything is going great, a diet trap is waiting around the corner to mess it all up by tricking you into giving away exactly what you want most—that thinner, healthier body.

This step is going to show you how to deal.

Let's face it—most diets just don't seem to be made with you in mind. They assume you have no social life, no appetite, no weird-looking food choices in the school cafeteria, and access to an unlimited supply of fresh veggies and low-fat cheese platters. Come on! We all know what it's really like: You eat whatever you can find lying around your parents' house, you choke down greasy cafeteria food for lunch, and you spend most of your free time hanging out at the diner or snacking at friends' houses. Not exactly ideal when you're trying to stick to a diet! Here are a few diet traps you may have run into before. Check off any that sound familiar to you.

❏ You stay up until midnight studying, so you can't wake up in time for breakfast.

❏ You get stuck with sixth-period lunch, so you're starving by the time you get to the cafeteria every day—and primed to overeat.

❏ You feel weird ordering a sugar-free frozen yogurt when your friends go for an ice cream run.

❏ You want to go for a walk, but your mom asks you to baby-sit for your little brother.

❏ You're about to leave for the gym when a friend calls and wants to hang out instead.

❏ Your mom cooks with a lot of butter, and she'd be mad if you didn't eat what she made.

❏ You have the first lunch period, so you're starving by the middle of the afternoon—and make a run for the candy machine.

❏ The biggest hangout in your town? Taco Bell. You just can't avoid it.

ZAP THE TRAPS

Diet traps fall into three major categories:

Unconscious Eating: Eating without paying attention

Eating Alarm Times: Specific times of day when you're most likely to overeat

Diet Busters: Foods or events that can throw a wrench in your diet routine

Like diet styles and patterns, these traps are individual. So in this step, you won't just get the 411 on diet traps—you'll find out which ones are most dangerous to you. Then you'll get the weapons to zap them out of your way.

 The fact is, anyone and everyone is vulnerable to diet traps. But anyone can beat them and get back on track to a diet that's automatic.

DIET TRAP #1: UNCONSCIOUS EATING

You're sitting in front of your computer, IMing a few friends. As you wait for replies, you munch on a box of cookies from the pantry. First it's just one. Then it's a few. Before you know it, the whole box is gone. Sound familiar?

Later, you plop down on the couch to watch TV, crunching on chips. Each time you take a handful, you think it'll be your last, but then suddenly you've grabbed another without even noticing it. You don't bother to read the label to see if they're worth the calories—after all, you're planning to stop any minute! Except that minute never comes, and you end up eating more than 600 calories' worth (or about five handfuls).

If you keep up this habit twice a week for a year, you'll end up with 8 extra pounds!

Unconscious eating doesn't mean chowing down while you have a concussion. And it doesn't mean eating while you're hypnotized. This diet trap rears its ugly head in two ways:

- Eating in a mindless way, like finishing those cookies in front of your computer...without even really *wanting* them. You can put away thousands of extra calories a week this way, without getting anything—like satisfaction or a full stomach—in return. What a waste!

- Eating foods without having any idea of the number of calories they're costing you. If you really saw how much your body was paying for that buttery bagel or extra-large muffin (that'll leave you hungry in half an hour, by the way), it would blow your mind!

Little Bites Mean a Lot

Whether it's unconscious eating in the kitchen or social eating at a party, nibbling here and there can add up. Don't think it can be that bad?

Passing Through the Kitchen

- 4 spoonfuls of ice cream from the freezer: *150 calories*
- 5 Lay's Classic potato chips: *40 calories*
- 1 Oreo Double Stuf cookie: *70 calories*
- 1 handful of trail mix: *174 calories*
- 1 Hershey's Kiss: *25 calories*
- 10 Rold Gold Classic Tiny Twists pretzels: *65 calories*
- 1 handful of raisins: *86 calories*

Cooking

- 1 slice of cheese: *100 calories*
- Crumbs from the bottom of a bag of cookies: *140 calories*
- 1 spoonful of cookie dough: *32 calories*
- 1 spoon of just the chocolate chips: *80 calories*
- Licking the peanut butter off a knife while making a sandwich: *95 calories*

Out and About

- 4 wheat crackers: *76 calories*
- 2 big handfuls of movie theater popcorn with butter: *168 calories*
- 1 bite of a hot dog at a baseball game: *48 calories*

"Stealing" Food

- 2 bites of the chocolate cake off your sister's plate: *117 calories*
- 10 fries from your friend's plate: *53 calories*
- 1 bite of a McDonald's cheeseburger: *40 calories*

Leftovers

- 2 bites of cold pizza: *77 calories*
- 3 bites of leftover Chinese food: *about 70 calories*

Drinks

- 1 gulp of OJ from the fridge: *28 calories*
- 1 sip of regular soda: *25 calories*

FIND YOUR UNCONSCIOUS-EATING PATTERNS

Think about some instances where you've eaten for reasons other than hunger. These can be as small as snacking during your favorite shows to pass the time, or as big as bingeing after someone has hurt you or made you angry. Be kind to yourself and tell the truth about your reasons for eating at these times. Then look for the pattern. The more in-depth you are about the reasons, the more helpful this exercise will be.

Times I ate when I wasn't hungry	Why I ate	Looking for patterns	What I've learned
Example: When my parents were getting divorced, I ate everything I could find in the pantry.	I kind of felt like overeating would get them to notice how miserable I was.	I tend to overeat when I want to let the world know I'm unhappy.	I need to find another way to deal with unhappiness that won't make things even worse.

Why the Calorie Coma?

You wouldn't buy a bunch of clothes you didn't really want. And you wouldn't buy a piece of clothing without knowing what it cost, would you? So why put something in your mouth without really wanting it, or knowing how much you're paying in calories and fat... *and pounds?*

Well, for one thing, it might be that you'd rather not know. Ignoring the calories going into your body may keep you in guilt-free la-la land. The problem there is that ignorance *isn't* bliss. Those calories will be hard to ignore when they show up on the scale.

Then there's the fact that you get certain benefits from unconscious eating—"perks" that you don't want to give up. To zap this trap, you've got to become a "diet detective" again—and figure out what those perks are. And to do that, you've got to know what kind of unconscious eater you are.

Uncover Your Eating Alter Ego

Most of us eat unconsciously. Here's a way to figure out *your* M.O. Circle the one that best applies to you.

Since these habits are unconscious, give each question some thought before answering. If more than one applies to you, circle that, too.

1. I'm most likely to binge on snack food when

   a. I'm watching TV or doing homework

   b. I'm at a party or gathering

   c. I'm upset or worried about something

   d. I haven't had enough to eat earlier in the day

2. If I had to give up snacking between meals, the first thing I'd wonder would be

   a. What am I going to eat while I do homework?

   b. What are my friends and I going to do without our Starbucks time?

   c. How am I going to cheer myself up?

   d. How am I going to make it to dinner?

3. At the movies I

   a. Always buy popcorn and a soda. It's part of the experience

   b. Don't buy snacks…but I always munch off someone else's when they offer

   c. Only buy a snack if it's been a rough week and I deserve it

   d. Buy a popcorn or nachos to keep me going till dinner

Mostly A's: The Entertainer

How many times have you been in front of the TV (or the movie screen), chowing on a relatively full bag of chips (or popcorn), and reached for another handful only to find your knuckles scraping the bottom of an empty bag? You've just consumed countless calories, and probably without really tasting them.

When people eat for entertainment, they're focused on more than one thing, and they often click into mindless gear and eat whatever is at their fingertips. It's a surefire way to gain unneeded pounds.

> ## ZAP THIS TRAP
>
> No matter what else you're doing, always stop to think about what you're eating and whether you really want it—or whether it's just a big waste. If snacking makes the experience sweeter or the studying easier, you don't have to give it up—just go for the option that's healthiest and lowest in calories: baby carrots, an orange, an apple, or a small bowl filled with a measured amount of pretzels or chips. (Put the rest of the bag back in the kitchen!)
>
> If you decide ahead of time to eat only a healthy amount, you'll be able to enjoy every bite, knowing you're treating yourself—and your body—right.

Mostly B's: Social Eater

You're sitting at your friend's house, chatting and punctuating your sentences by chomping on the snacks on the coffee table.... You're at the mall with your pals, and you stop at Starbucks to talk over sips of tall lattes.... You're at a party, and your hand is constantly finding its way to a corn chip.

If you oversnack socially, you're not alone! People use food to calm their social nerves, to have something to do while they talk, to make the person who provided the food feel appreciated...or simply because other people are doing it.

But remember, if you've set up a great way to avoid the doughnuts in your parents' pantry, you're only canceling out that effort when you dig into a bag of Krispy Kremes someone's brought to school to share, or a bowl of Doritos in your friend's living room.

ZAP THIS TRAP

Before you cut down, keep track of what you're nibbling on socially. The more you do this, the more your awareness will become automatic. Then...

- Seek out the lowest-calorie options at your hangout spots.
- Skip free samples at the mall; skip the free, fatty snacks at parties or gatherings.
- Don't ever feel you have to pick from your friend's plate (or even your own) because you don't want to "waste" food.
- Don't feel obligated to eat a bunch of snacks just because someone offered or provided them. Your body's fitness is more important.
- Curb your urge to take a slurp of soda at the mall or at parties.

SIZE UP STARBUCKS AND DUNKIN' DONUTS

If you're like a lot of people I know, you love to hang out at Starbucks with your friends. But be careful—a Frappuccino light can have about as many calories as a McDonald's shake! And just one piece of coffee crumb cake and a fancy Frappuccino with whipped cream at Starbucks (1,180 calories total) adds up to more than a Big Mac, medium fries, and a soda (1,060 calories). Here are a few hints to help you make better choices the next time you have your cup of java.

STARBUCKS REDUCED-FAT BLUEBERRY COFFEE CAKE VS. CHOCOLATE-FILLED CROISSANT

Surprisingly, the croissant at 350 calories is a better choice than the 380-calorie coffee cake. Plus, the coffee cake is made with trans fat and has 500 milligrams of sodium.

FIT TIP Just because it's reduced-fat or is made with yogurt doesn't mean it's healthy. Starbucks' lemon yogurt Bundt cake is certainly not a healthy choice at 350 calories.

DUNKIN' DONUTS STRAWBERRY-CHEESE DANISH VS. CHOCOLATE-FROSTED DOUGHNUT

The doughnut wins. The Danish (250 calories) isn't bad, considering other dieting nightmares, but the doughnut has "only" 200 calories. Doughnuts aren't diet food, but, if you avoid the cake and cream-filled varieties, they might be better than many muffins, scones, and Danishes. Even a jelly doughnut has just 210 calories; compare that to a Starbucks crumb cake at a whopping 670 calories.

FIT TIP Cake doughnuts have twice as much fat as yeast doughnuts and are higher in calories. Look at the difference between a Dunkin' Donuts chocolate-frosted yeast doughnut (200 calories) and the chocolate-frosted cake doughnut (360 calories).

STARBUCKS WHITE-CHOCOLATE MACADAMIA-NUT COOKIE VS. RASPBERRY-AND-CREAM-CHEESE-FILLED CROISSANT

The cookie (470 calories) has almost twice as many calories as the croissant (260 calories).

FIT TIP For baked goods, your best bet is typically biscotti, at around 110 to 150 calories.

DUNKIN' DONUTS EGG-AND-CHEESE ENGLISH MUFFIN SANDWICH VS. REDUCED-CARB BAGEL

The English muffin sandwich (280 calories) wins. The reduced-carb bagel starts out with 380 calories, and if you add cream cheese (190 calories for 2 ounces), you'll have eaten 570 calories before you even get to your coffee.

Even a Starbucks sesame bagel has 440 calories (not to mention toppings)—the same as their raspberry scone.

FIT TIP Scoop out the inside of the bagel to save up to half the calories. Additionally, try low-fat cream cheese (110 calories per 2 ounces). A better breakfast would be low-fat yogurt or a cup of sliced fruit, which has 44 calories. It might be the best deal of all.

DUNKIN' DONUTS COFFEE COOLATTA WITH SKIM MILK VS. STARBUCKS ESPRESSO FRAPPUCCINO LIGHT

The espresso Frappuccino light (140 calories per 16 ounces) wins by 30 calories. The Coolatta with skim milk has 170 calories per 16 ounces.

FIT TIP Choose skim milk or, at the very least, low-fat milk. The Coolatta with cream has 180 more calories than the Coolatta with skim.

CHOCOLATE MILK OR HOT CHOCOLATE VS. STARBUCKS CHANTICO DRINKING CHOCOLATE

The Chantico at Starbucks has 390 calories and 21 grams of fat (10 of them saturated) per 6 ounces. Sixteen ounces of chocolate milk/hot chocolate, on the other hand, contains 340 calories and 15 grams of fat (8 saturated). Try 12 ounces of nonfat chocolate milk or hot chocolate (no whipped cream) for 190 calories.

FIT TIP Have regular coffee with skim milk and Splenda, and if you're at Starbucks, get one of those little dark chocolate squares at the counter (60 calories). Or try the sugar-free flavored syrups for no calories.

STARBUCKS ICED TAZO CHAI TEA LATTE VS. DUNKIN' DONUTS CARAMEL SWIRL LATTE WITH SOY MILK

At 200 calories per 12 ounces, the chai wins—you get 2 more ounces and it still has fewer calories than the 10-ounce latte (210 calories). Tea without sugar and milk has virtually no calories, but when you make it fancy, the calories add up. Take a look at Starbucks' Tazo chai creme Frappuccino blended tea (16 ounces), at 510 calories.

FIT TIP Try herbal tea—it's flavored and has no calories.

ESPRESSO VS. CAPPUCCINO VS. LATTE VS. CAFÉ AU LAIT

At 5 calories per ounce, a shot of espresso is your best deal. A 16-ounce Starbucks cappuccino (an espresso with steamed milk and a layer of foam) has 150 calories. A latte is an espresso with more steamed milk than a cappuccino, also topped with foam—it has 260 calories per 16 ounces. Café au lait is a one-to-one mix of coffee and steamed milk, and 16 ounces has 140 calories.

FIT TIP Skip the whipped cream and save at least 100 calories and as much as a quarter of a day's worth of saturated fat.

Mostly C's: Comfort or Stress Eater

You had a fight with someone you care about, you bombed a test, you're overwhelmed with schoolwork or your part-time job—you are *stressed out*. Where can you find relief?

How about in a slice of cheesecake, an order of fries, or a pint of ice cream? These foods are always quick to the rescue in our times of need. And comfort eaters gravitate toward them without really thinking about it.

You turn to comfort foods for all sorts of reasons.

- **Emotional:** You might connect certain foods with good memories, like of someone taking care of you.
- **Biological:** "Comfort foods" can actually cause the release of happy brain chemicals, such as endorphins and serotonin, that calm and soothe you.

The problem is, these foods are generally high in carbohydrates, sugar, and fat. Basically, you go to the wrong food for the right reasons.

Each of us has our unique version of comfort food. For me, it's a hot bowl of spaghetti like my mom used to make. What are some of yours?

_____

_____

_____

_____

_____

_____

Mostly D's: The Delayed Feeder

How often have you gone without eating until you were ready to devour everything in your kitchen? You skip a meal here and there because you're not that hungry, and you figure, "Hey, skipping calories—that's gotta be a bonus!" At lunch you pick at your food while you're busy talking or studying or cramming in some extra homework.

When delayed feeders finally feed, they feed _big_. Remember the _starvation trap?_ Delayed feeders undergo a micro version of that every day. When they finally eat, they're not thinking about the calories they're consuming, because their body is

America's Comfort Food Faves
1. Potato chips
2. Ice cream
3. Cookies
4. Pizza or Pasta/Chocolate (tie)
5. Steak/Burgers

(Source: The Food and Brand Lab at the University of Illinois at Urbana-Champaign)

Five Ways to Soothe the Soul and Still Slim Down

Instead of: *Brownies, 2 oz. (227 calories)*
Try: *Fat-free chocolate pudding, ½ cup (130 calories)*
Savings: *97 calories*

Instead of: *Doughnut, 1.5 oz. (310 calories)*
Try: *Low-fat muffin, 1.5 oz. (160 calories)*
Savings: *150 calories*

Instead of: *Cheese pizza, 1 medium slice (280 calories)*
Try: *Pita bread pizza with skim mozzarella (216 calories)*
Savings: *64 calories*

Instead of: *Spaghetti and meatballs, 3 cups (770 calories)*
Try: *Spaghetti and turkey meatballs, 3 cups (630 calories)*
Savings: *140 calories*

Chicken soup: *No revisions necessary—enjoy!*

Fill In Your Own Soul-Soothing Food Alternatives Here

Instead of: _____(favorite comfort food)

Try: _____(a comfort alternative)

Instead of: _____

Try: _____

Instead of: _____

Try: _____

Instead of: _____

Try: _____

screaming, "Feed me!" loud enough to drown out any other thoughts. And the real kicker is that delayed feasts usually consist of foods that are high in fat and calories.

ZAP THIS TRAP

Make time to eat. Don't skip meals or wait too long between meals (keep healthy snacks like a small handful of nuts, some cut-up veggies, or low-cal cereals in your backpack just in case). Skipping meals may seem like a diet shortcut, but in no time it will become a diet detour—because your body will simply rebel.

And I've said it before, but I can't stress it enough: Skipping breakfast will most likely make you *gain weight*—so even if you're rushed or not that hungry, figure out a way to get a little something healthy in your belly before that first class.

A Last Word About Unconscious Eating

You've almost mastered this diet trap. But before we move on...

The number one way to battle unconscious eating is to...eat consciously!

Q: How do I eat consciously?

A: • Be aware of what you eat and when.

• Be aware of the calories (and the fat, carbs, and protein) in what you're eating.

• When you do want to overeat, ask yourself why, and have a few good reasons why not ready to go.

As I've said before, eating sweets and snacks isn't always bad. But when you eat them, make sure you're really getting your calories' worth. Eat because you enjoy the taste of the food, not out of mindless habit; know what you're getting; and always stop when you feel satisfied.

Remember, it's these little changes that count. Once you make them, eating consciously will become automatic.

AVOID THE FLASHING NEON SIGN

As soon as we decide to diet, we come up with lists of foods we can't eat. We might as well put up a neon sign flashing, "EAT—EAT—EAT," because any time you try telling yourself not to do something...that's exactly what you'll find yourself doing.

DIET TRAP #2: EATING ALARM TIMES

When do you get the worst munchies? Late at night? After school? Almost all of us have a specific time of day that's dangerous to our diet.

What is the one time of day you tend to overeat most? Basically, what is your weakest time of day, foodwise? Think carefully, and check *one:*

❑ Breakfast time (5:00 A.M.–9:00 A.M.)

❑ Mid-morning munchies (9:00 A.M.–11:00 A.M.)

❑ Lunchtime (11:00 A.M.–2:30 P.M.)

❑ After-school snack attack (2:30 P.M.–5:00 P.M.)

❑ Dinnertime (5:00 P.M.–8:00 P.M.)

❑ Prime-time TV (8:00 P.M.–11:00 P.M.)

❑ Late-night nibbles (11:00 P.M. until...)

The box you checked is your **Eating Alarm Time, or what I like to call your EAT.** EATs are deadly diet traps, and here's why: At these times, day in and day out, you pack on unneeded calories, like clockwork.

Bad EATs

Three hundred fifty calories a day (the average amount we eat during Eating Alarm Times) can add up to more than 30 pounds a year!

Q: Okay, fine. Now that I know my EAT, I can just promise myself I won't overeat at that time, right?

A: Not so fast! Guarding against EATs is not quite *that* simple! You'll still *want* to eat at the same time every day, even when you promise yourself you won't. The good thing about Eating Alarm Times, though, is that they're pretty specific. Concentrating on one time of day means you can narrow your focus—and make big changes in your weight. Just use these few easy tactics and overcome your EATs for real.

ZAP THIS TRAP

GET READY

Since you know you're going to be tempted to overeat at certain times, have Calorie Bargain snacks at the ready. And be careful—carrots and celery might not always cut it as a replacement for ice cream, doughnuts, and Doritos. So, if you normally eat chips while sitting in front of prime-time TV, make sure to come up with a variety of alternatives that'll keep you satisfied, even on your most splurge-worthy days.

Come up with five of your own replacement snack ideas—basically, Calorie Bargains for your EATs. Remember, these are supposed to be permanent changes—so make sure these snacks are good, tasty substitutions that are lower in calories than what you would normally eat:

_____

_____

_____

_____

_____

Get Active

If your EAT habit is to munch your way through weekend mornings or downtime after school, you might want to try finding another activity to fill the time (it doesn't always work, but it's a suggestion—and it doesn't hurt to try). You could:

- Set aside a time to write, draw, or read.
- Take a class in something fun at your local community center.
- Teach yourself a cool skill (you can learn guitar, drawing, and lots of other stuff on the Internet, from a book at the library, or from a CD-ROM).
- Make a regular exercise date with a buddy.
- Take a long walk.
- Shoot hoops.
- Work out.

Anything will do, as long as it entertains you and keeps you busy.

Get Planning

Use this worksheet to come up with your own ideas for beating the EATs. Then come back to this page whenever you're facing an Eating Alarm Time and don't know what to do.

Example:

My Eating Alarm Time is: *The late afternoon, because I get home from school at 2:00 and have four hours to kill until dinner.*

Adjustments I can make (with the foods I eat, or the stuff I choose to occupy my time):

1. *Pick a different "TV snack," like sugar-free pudding or Jell-O.*

2. *Don't bring the bag of nacho chips into the living room. If I have to keep running out of the room to grab a chip, I won't be as likely to eat half the bag.*

3. *Watch TV in the basement, so I have to run upstairs if I want food.*

4. *Join a club or have other activities after school, so I'm not sitting at home thinking about what to eat.*

5. *Use that time to take a walk or ride my bike or finish my chores—something that'll keep me moving.*

6. *Make myself a healthy snack like apples and a smudge of peanut butter, so I don't mindlessly pick at chips and ice cream and cookies and leftovers.*

7. *Check the serving size on the bag of chips, and only eat one serving instead of half the bag. I'll put the chips in a bowl, put the bag back in the closet, and leave the kitchen before I start eating.*

Your turn:

My Eating Alarm Time is: _____

Adjustments I can make (with the foods I eat, or the stuff I choose to occupy my time):

1._____

2._____

3._____

4._____

5._____

DIET TRAP #3: DIET BUSTERS!

We've all been there. Our diets are chugging along right on track. Our pants are getting looser, we're looking better and better, and then...*pow!* Something knocks us off course.

So far in this step you've acquired some major skills for tackling eating habits you can predict and prepare for. But you and I both know that not every obstacle is so predictable. Some diet traps appear out of the blue. And no matter how well we plan, we can't seem to avoid walking into them. I call these traps Diet Busters.

Diet Busters can be:

- Certain foods that have a powerful effect on you
- Certain situations and events that knock you off the diet track

But even though you can't always see Diet Busters coming, you are still totally capable of keeping them in check.

To do that, let's take them one by one.

Diet-Buster Foods

Certain foods seem to have magic powers. You get within a couple of feet of them and the angel sitting on your right shoulder (the one telling you to stick to your healthy routine) starts to drool. You turn to your willpower for backup, but it seems to have called in sick. And then, well...you give in.

I can say with *complete certainty* that this has happened to *everyone* who has ever tried to lose weight and keep it off. But guess what? No matter how many times you've been seduced by nachos or s'mores, this section will put *you* in the driver's seat—instead of the foods that tempt you. And, believe it or not, you can face *any* Diet-Buster food and come out on top.

Think of three foods that are irresistible to you. What foods are they? What makes them so hard to turn down? Write them below.

Example: *I love loaded nachos, and I always end up scarfing the whole plate!*

_____

_____

_____

Next, come up with three ways to deal with those foods.

THREE WAYS TO TRIM DOWN A TEMPTING FOOD

1. **Shave your portion.** Would half a brownie be enough to satisfy your sweet tooth?
2. **Leave off the extra calories.** Will you be satisfied without the side of fries, the coleslaw, whipped cream, or mayo?
3. **Think bargains.** Here's yet another opportunity to create some Calorie Bargains. Can you get it grilled instead of fried? Or with marinara instead of cream sauce?

Write your ideas below:

Example: *I can ask for the sour cream and guacamole to be left off my nachos and arrange to split the plate with a friend or two. That way I still get my favorite meal but I don't overdo it. I could also get something else now and make my famous low-cal nachos at home for my next meal.*

Food 1 _____

Food 2 _____

Food 3 _____

Diet-Buster Moments

During Diet-Buster moments, you tend to slip up, no matter how much you mean to stay strong. These moments differ from person to person, but they include events like birthdays, holidays, parties, family vacations, school gatherings, school trips, summer camp—you name it.

Diet-Buster moments often bring disappointment in yourself and lower your confidence—the very thing you need to control your weight. Not to mention, these "minor slipups" add up weightwise.

Life Changes Bust Diets, Too

Aside from travel, almost any major life-changing event can be a big Diet Buster. Here are just a few you might have already experienced.

Moving is stressful on lots of levels. For one, it takes effort, and all that work can cut into breakfast, lunch, and dinnertime and screw up your routine, not to mention put healthy eating on the back burner. And as if that weren't enough, it can be so emotionally draining that you may turn to food for comfort.

Divorce has a big misery factor. If your parents are in the middle of one, it can get in the way of your routine and your emotional well-being, and that can be rough on your diet.

A breakup can *also* have a big misery factor. You may turn to food to console yourself, or you may give up on your healthy eating habits altogether—what's the point?

Loss can also mess up your eating habits. If you lose a family member, a friend, even a family pet, sadness and self-doubt can make the fridge your favorite friendly companion. And once again, grief can wreak havoc on routine, making it hard to stick to what you know you should eat.

But Wait, There's More....

Here are a few more classic Diet-Buster moments that might ring a bell....

Weekends

Have you ever said to yourself, "I work hard at school, I'm busy, and I stick to my diet all week long. On weekends I deserve a break!"

According to the latest research, people tend to eat an extra 115 calories a day on Friday, Saturday, and Sunday...which adds up to an extra 345 calories per week. That can mean up to an extra 5 pounds in a year!

Danger Zones

Everyone has food associations with certain places and activities. Does a day at the beach *need* to be accompanied by ice cream on the boardwalk? Do outings with friends seem to call for a splurge? Whatever it is, for many of us there is a circumstance, situation, or event that inevitably causes us to "bust" our diets.

Party Time

On special occasions like birthdays, big family dinners, weddings, New Year's bashes, and just regular old parties, we love to eat high-calorie and high-fat foods—and of course we love to think it's no big deal.

Eating on big social occasions is a major Diet Buster, and here are a few reasons why.

- We eat with *those people who eat and never gain weight.* It makes us think we can do the same thing.

- *Seeing others eat makes us want to eat, too*—and, more important, overeat. In my family, it's a big joke that when we eat breakfast, our minds are already on lunch. In situations where everybody's in on the action, it's hard not to overeat.

- We eat around *"food pushers,"* people who are famous for sayings like "How can one bite hurt?"; "Live a little, it's a party!"; and "You look great—have another slice!"

The truth is that not finding excuses to Diet Bust at parties can be the best gift you can give yourself. Keeping control—and having a great body to show for it—will be reason enough to celebrate.

Know Your Own Diet-Buster Moments...and Zap 'Em

Now I'm going to ask you to identify your top Diet-Buster moments—the circumstances, situations, or events that are, and probably always have been, most difficult for you. Once you know what they are, you'll be able to figure out how to control them.

Do You Indulge on "Special" Days?

Well, let's do the math. Let's say you have about fifty "special days" a year. Let's say you eat about 500 extra calories (which isn't that hard—it's about one piece of cake or one bowl of ice cream) on those days. The result? About 25,000 calories...or more than 7 pounds a year! Who would have thought?

Check off the situations below in which you find it most difficult to keep control and stick to your diet.

- ❏ Holidays
- ❏ Family gatherings
- ❏ Parties and birthdays
- ❏ Vacations
- ❏ School trips
- ❏ Weekends

Have there been any other events that have been hard on your diet? Write them below.

_____

_____

_____

_____

_____

_____

_____

Everything you've checked or written above is a **personal Diet-Buster moment**.

Now it's time to brainstorm. For each item you've marked, come up with three ways you can take control and protect your diet.

Example: *My number one Diet Buster is holidays. On Christmas my mom lays out about twenty different kinds of cookies. So here's my solution.*

Diet Buster #1: Holidays

1. *Make sure the kitchen is stocked with plenty of great-tasting, low-calorie snacks that I can nibble on, so hunger doesn't add to the temptation.*

2. *Let my mom know that the cookies are hard on my diet, and ask her if there's an adjustment we can make, like keeping them in the pantry where people can get them if they want, but where they aren't in my face.*

3. *I can even ask Mom if she'd be willing to bake an additional, lower-cal kind of cookie, too.*

Now it's your turn. Fill in three ways to take control for each Diet Buster you checked or wrote down.

Diet Buster #1:

1._____

2._____

3._____

Diet Buster #2:

1._____

2._____

3._____

Diet Buster #3:

1._____

2._____

3._____

Diet Buster #4:

1._____

2._____

3._____

Diet Buster #5:

1._____

2._____

3._____

Diet Buster #6:

1._____

2._____

3._____

On the Road Again

Handling the holidays is one thing, but what about when you're totally out of your element? Here are a few tips to keep you on the thin track when you're away from home:

Food for Thought

If your family (or the group you're with) always stops for fast food, have your low-cal fast-food alternatives—and maybe this book—handy. If you have to eat at restaurants, always go for grilled or steamed dishes, watch the sides (ask for them to be left off if you're willing), and stay away from heavy dressings.

Think Ahead

Pack sandwiches and snacks (apples, low-fat yogurt, veggies (or any other Calorie Bargain snacks) the night before you travel, even if it's by plane. (Don't get caught starving—a couple of those airplane peanut bags can be deadly.) And wherever you're going, *be sure* to pack a water bottle. When you get dehydrated, you'll feel hungrier than you really are.

Virtual Fitness

Most hotels (and homes, for that matter, if you're staying with relatives or friends) have DVD or VHS players. There are plenty of great exercise videos to buy on the Internet (collagevideo.com), or you can rent one at your library or even online from netflix.com. Wait until your travel mates go to breakfast or down to the pool and then go for it. You can join them in 20 minutes.

Take a Hike

Going for a walk and exploring is a great way to take a break from the group, see a new place, and fit in some physical activity. Ask the hotel concierge or a relative (if you're visiting) for hiking trails, great walks, even shopping malls—any place where you can stretch your legs. For a twist, rent or borrow a bike.

Mistakes Happen—Keep Moving!

You wouldn't expect to get 100% on every test or be the best soccer player, the fastest runner, the most talented artist, *and* the most gifted writer in your school, would you? Nobody's perfect! So why expect to be perfect at losing weight?

In Steps 4 and 5, you saw that diet traps and diet patterns can be major stumbling blocks on the way to weight loss. But a lot of times, instead of getting "back on the horse," we use our diet mistakes as opportunities to give up on ourselves and eat whatever we want.

That's why I want you to remember something I said at the beginning of Step 4: **Big mistakes are big opportunities to learn...and succeed!**

By remembering this, you'll be able to keep a clear head in the face of Diet-Buster moments and your most stubborn diet patterns. And then you'll be able to use everything you know now to overcome them so that the next time around, it won't be your diet mistakes that are in control, but you. Because you've learned how to turn defeat into victory...and made it automatic.

WHAT YOU JUST GOT

In this step you realized that it's not just about food, it's also about you. What you do every day, the people you see, the places you go, and where you live—these things can all have an impact on your weight. Knowing your diet enemies puts you way ahead of the game. Now you know how to prevent diet traps from sabotaging your diet.

NEXT UP

If you think getting physical is for somebody else, think again! Step 6 will show you how to get active to shed pounds, *even if* you think exercise is a dirty word.

STEP 6 Get Physical

THE *E* WORD

Let's talk about the dreaded *E* word. *Exercise.*

From here on out, I'm not going to mention it again. Why? Because for lots of people, the *E* word conjures up visions of flat-abbed, gym-suit-wearing athletes jumping rope, running sweaty laps around the track, and doing long rounds of sit-ups in the gym. Workout junkies and perfect bodies just aren't what this step is about.

So what *is* it about? Well, it's simple. It's about using physical activity to jump-start your diet and help you lose weight *faster*—without gym suits, a jump rope, or even sweat. **And actually, it's as simple as taking a walk**.

WALK, DON'T RUN, AWAY

I know what you're thinking. Or at least I can guess. You're waiting for the catch. Well, if you're anything like I was in high school, you *hate* the *E* word.

True or False: Exercising for 10 minutes three times a day instead of 30 minutes all at once is just as effective.

True. But keep in mind: Some people do fine increasing their activity in small doses, fitting in 10 minutes here and there. Others need to "get it out of the way" all at once.

But here's the only thing I can say to that: You don't have to do stuff you hate to make a huge difference to your diet through physical activity.

Get ready to forget what you know about getting physical.

WHY GET PHYSICAL?

Q: I hate physical activity of any kind! Give me a good reason why I shouldn't skip this step and just diet.

A: Actually, I can give you *five* good reasons. But first, I'll admit it: It probably *is* easier to *skip* calories than to burn them off by walking (after all, one large bite of a candy bar can equal 100 calories, or 25 minutes of walking). But now here's a question for you: What's keeping you from doing both?

> If 3,500 calories equals one pound of fat, burning just an additional 100 calories per day means losing about 10 pounds in one year!

Great Reason #1: You'll lose weight faster!! (Because you'll burn more calories.)

Great Reason #2: You'll speed up your metabolism by doing strength training, which ups the number of calories you burn *even when you're doing absolutely nothing!*

Great Reason #3: According to the experts, physical activity makes your skin clearer and brighter, gives you more energy, helps your mood and self-esteem, and boosts your brainpower—and then there are all the lifelong body benefits going on under the surface. Oh, and no more wheezing in gym class! Oh, wait, that's six reasons!

Great Reason #4: It'll help you keep off the weight you've already lost.

Great Reason #5: Um, you might actually enjoy it.
   Stranger things have happened.

With so many perks—and when it's so easy—why *wouldn't* it be worth it?

REASONS WHY WE DON'T DO IT

Before we get to the many ways you can make getting physical work for you, let's face up to the facts: Even with all the miraculous benefits I've mentioned, it's still tempting to shy away from physical activity. You may decide...

I'm Not Cut Out to Get Physical

When you're not exactly a physically active person, believing you can get organized and then actually *doing it* is tough. As I've said before, it's hard to believe we're capable of things we haven't accomplished yet. But if you read the simple strategies I'll outline in this step, you'll see that *this* is something you *can* do—so well it becomes automatic.

There's Too Much in My Way

- There's no place to do it in your area; it's too expensive to join a gym, a pool, or go to the beach; you haven't got a safe area to walk around near your house; there's no place to walk, period—these are all *environmental* barriers.

- You haven't got the time, you're embarrassed, you really don't feel like it—these are all *emotional* barriers.

But don't sweat it—barriers were made to be broken.

BLASTING YOUR BARRIERS

Look for Your Opportunities

Does your neighborhood have public or private recreation facilities (like public swimming pools, parks, walking trails, bike paths, activity centers, etc.)? List the ones you can think of.

_____

_____

_____

_____

_____

_____

_____

Are they in good condition? Can you see yourself using them?

Does your school have any facilities you can use on weekends or after school?

Does your neighborhood shopping mall have any walking programs available?

Do you have safety concerns about using your local recreation facilities? What about walking in your neighborhood? Can you think of any ways you could deal with these issues?

True or False: To burn the most calories, don't eat before you work out.

False. In fact, the opposite is true. If you don't eat, you probably won't have the energy to work out for as long as if you ate something healthy first.

Think Outside the Box

If the above questions don't turn up any leads—because your neighborhood's not safe or it's severely lacking in the recreation department—don't worry. The rest of this step will help you find physical opportunities where you least expect them.

BRAINSTORM

If you can think of any parks, walking trails, or bike paths that *are* safe and that you'd be allowed and *willing* to use, write them below. You can also try logging on to traillink.com or pedbikeinfo.org to find some areas near you that you may not know about.

1._____

2._____

3._____

4. _____

5._____

6._____

Don't Chance It

Don't leave your increase in physical activity up to chance—doing that just increases your chances of running up against barriers. Make it easy: Create automatic opportunities like the ones I'm about to give you.

True or False: If you don't work out for at least 60 minutes, you shouldn't bother.

False. The bottom line is that some is *always* better than none.

SNEAK IT, DON'T SWEAT IT

Use these suggestions to inspire you to sneak physical activity into your day, then look for your own opportunities: *That's the way to make it automatic.*

Mow It: Don't wait for your parents to beg you to do it (or demand it)—you'll burn 175 calories each half hour you mow, and you'll earn brownie points to boot.

Use the Pet: Take the time to go for a long walk with your dog each and every day. A 30-minute promenade with the pooch burns up to 80 calories.

Wash the Car: Here's another way to impress your parents and burn calories at the same time: Wash the family car(s) by hand. Half an hour burns about 140 calories.

Ditch Driving: If you drive to your friends' houses, to stores, or anywhere else, consider whether they're close enough for you to walk. Walking burns 160–260 calories per hour.

Dish It Out: Washing the dishes and cleaning the house for an hour will burn more than 100 calories.

Get a Green Thumb: Get out the shovel and start your own garden. And while you're at it, try growing some healthy food! Thirty minutes of gardening burns about 160 calories.

Get Shopping: Go to the mall with the intention of walking around and window-shopping for an hour twice a week. Leave your ATM card at home!

 If you're already doing some of these things, great. But remember, you have to *increase* your activities to *increase* the calories you're burning—so aim to step it up.

AMAZING, ULTRA-FABULOUS WALKING!

It's hard to convince people that doing something as simple as taking a walk can really make a dent in their weight. Personally, as a teen, I never thought much of walking (except that it got me where I wanted to go)... until I realized its amazing potential.

Here's what's so amazing about it.

- It's painless.
- You won't feel self-conscious doing it.
- You can do it anywhere.
- You already know how.
- You can use it to do other stuff at the same time: shop, visit friends, check out a new place, explore nature, whatever.

Oh, and if you're still not convinced walking is worth much, get this:

You only burn about 20% more calories when you run a mile than you do when you walk a mile. Not bad, huh?

The bottom line is: **Walking is one of the most important life-changing physical activities there is**.

Q: I walk for half an hour every day, but I never break a sweat! Does this mean I'm not burning any calories?

A: Nope. In fact, easy physical activity burns calories just as effectively as the high-intensity kind (according to a study reported by the University of Pittsburgh). You don't need to sweat or even walk *fast* in order to lose weight.

WATCH YOUR WALK

If you really want to get the most from walking, you might want to get a **pedometer** (available online and at most sporting goods stores). A pedometer's basic function is to count the steps you take throughout the day. It contains an internal lever that's triggered by your hip movement, counting each step.

Why use a pedometer? Because monitoring yourself helps you become aware of what your body is capable of doing. And once you're in tune with your body's capabilities, you can increase the number of steps you take in a day. Plus, it's easy to use and you'll barely notice it on your belt.

So how many steps are enough? The average person accumulates 3,000 to 5,000 steps per day. The goal is to increase your number of steps per day to about 10,000.

A WEEK IN YOUR LIFE

So, now that you have some tips for working the physical into your life, let's get busy. The best way to discover your activity opportunities is to look at what you typically do in a week...and then look for places to inject the physical. What's a typical week like for you? Describe how you spend your day: What time do you get up? How do you get to school? What kind of stuff do you do after school? What about on the weekends? The more details, the better.

On weekdays I usually...

_____

_____

_____

_____

_____

On weekends I . . .

_____

_____

_____

_____

_____

Now take a look at what you wrote and brainstorm the ways (big or small! Maybe even *all* small! Whatever!) you can work in the physical. What seems manageable and doable—something you can do automatically every day without fail? Instead of lying on the couch before dinner watching *Friends* reruns, can you go for a walk or a bike ride? Or do some strength training moves while you're watching the show? Can you walk the mall for an hour on Saturdays and Sundays? Use the tips provided throughout this step for ideas.

Combine It
Try to come up with ways to combine extra activity with stuff you already like to do. For instance, why not watch *The O.C.* while you're on the stationary bike or treadmill (if you have one)? Other ideas: Take yoga classes with a friend you wish you had more time to see, or start a dog-walking business and burn calories and earn extra cash all at once!

_____

_____

_____

_____

_____

_____

_____

WANNA KICK IT UP A NOTCH?

Hey, I said getting physical was as easy as taking a walk, and I meant it. If you're not ready to bring it to another level, that's fine. You've already picked up some great ideas, and if you use them, you'll definitely see results.

But if a walk can do wonders, think of what stepping it up can do!

CALORIE BURNING PER MINUTE OF ACTIVITY			
	Easy	**Moderate**	**Brisk/Fast**
Walking	4 cal./min.	4.5 cal./min.	5 cal./min.
Biking	7 cal./min.	11 cal./min.	13.5 cal./min.
Running	9 cal./min.	13 cal./min.	15 cal./min.

PUSH A LITTLE MORE...
AND PUSH AWAY THE POUNDS

On the next page I've listed some ideas for more intense activities that can give you more intense weight loss. Why not check off the ones that sound doable?

Remember, the more appealing the activity is to you, the more likely you are to stick to it—so focus on the ones you think you could enjoy. (But remember to be open-minded. I hated running until I started to listen to good music while I burned calories.)

True or False: Exercising makes you eat right.

False. Developing a better diet is something you've got to do on purpose.

- ❏ Badminton
- ❏ Basketball
- ❏ Dancing
- ❏ Rock climbing
- ❏ Rowing
- ❏ Skateboarding
- ❏ Soccer
- ❏ Tennis
- ❏ Baseball/Softball
- ❏ Biking (mountain, road, or dirt)
- ❏ Hiking
- ❏ Rollerblading
- ❏ Running
- ❏ Skiing
- ❏ Swimming
- ❏ Yoga

Did I miss a few? Write in any other activities you might be willing to try. Don't be afraid to think outside the box!

_____

_____

_____

_____

Now, of the above, which ones do you think you could do automatically, a few times a week, without fail? Put a star next to them, and then try to work those in on a regular basis. And remember, the cool thing about getting physical is that every ounce of effort pays off, every time, without fail.

PSYCH YOURSELF UP

When you're just starting out, getting a physical routine can involve hits and misses—and it's easy to get frustrated. Here's how to psych yourself up to get going and stick with it.

Slow and Steady Wins the Race: If you've never been physically active before, start out slowly—_don't overdo it_. You really need to cut yourself some slack so that you don't get exhausted and discouraged. And don't worry if you miss a day here and there—especially at first.

Have Fun: Give yourself time and room to experiment, and leeway to mix and match your activities. Having trouble finding the perfect fit? Until you do, at least tide yourself over with an activity that doesn't push you to hide under your bed.

Keep Your Eye on the Ball: Don't "take your eye off the ball" by "rewarding yourself" for physical activity. No reward will be big enough to motivate you for very long, and the *right* activity should be motivation enough. But hey, if you *really* need rewards to get you moving, try to use them only in the beginning. And whatever you do, don't reward yourself with food!

Make It Social: Working out with others makes it more likely you'll stick to a routine, and it's probably more fun. If you feel comfortable, find a workout buddy or enroll in a class at the local Y.

Make Your Plan: Decide when you're going to start getting more physical—like today! (Step 10 will help you pin this down.) And just remember, one of the most important parts of any plan is flexibility. As I've said, don't be too strict with your plan, your time, or yourself: Be ready and willing to roll with whatever changes come along!

DIET BONUS Get Fancy—Try Strength Training

For every pound of muscle tissue you gain through strength training, you burn an additional 30 to 50 calories per day. That's 18,250 calories per year, or about 5.2 pounds!

Wanna give it a try? After all, some people who hate other kinds of workouts love strength training, so it may turn out to be something you want to work into your weekly routine.

Q: But I don't belong to a gym—I can't afford something like that—and I'd hate to work out surrounded by a bunch of people, anyway. Can I still do strength training?

A: Yes! Workouts are easy to do at home, and you can get a dumbbell set for less than $20 at your local sporting goods store.

Q: My friend says strength training can make you gain weight! Is she right?

A: Strength training does build muscle, and muscles add weight. But remember that muscles help you burn calories, so they actually help you lose weight in the long run. Not to mention that muscles make your body look good.

WHAT YOU JUST GOT

To really succeed at getting the body you want, you've got to figure out what activities you love and stick with them. You've got to increase your activity *gradually,* in a way you enjoy, whether it's walking, biking, gardening, or working out at a gym. Do it because it feels good...and make it automatic.

NEXT UP

You know how to eat, how to motivate, how to get active... but there are still stubborn excuses lurking around every corner, threatening to keep you from kicking your thinner, fitter self into action. Get ready, get set for...Excuse Busters!

True or False: Muscle turns to fat when you don't get enough physical activity.

False. Muscle is muscle and fat is fat. What happens is that your muscles shrink and your fat increases, so you think the muscle has turned to fat.

STEP 7 Excuse Busters!

EXCUSES, EXCUSES, EXCUSES

Maybe your family is the opposite of supportive. Maybe your friends are always tempting you to eat. Or maybe it has nothing to do with people: Your schedule is too packed for you to focus on fat, you don't have anywhere to work out, you don't have good shoes for walking, you're just not an organized person...so you can't organize a diet.

If you're like most people, you use excuses and blame at least some of the time to let yourself off the hook. That's okay: It's natural; we all do it. But the fact is:

 When it comes down to it, *we* are the only ones responsible for our food choices.

Does that sound preachy? That's not really the point, I promise. *Here's* the point, and it's actually good news. **If you are the only one responsible for your weight, you have the power to change it**.

Hey, let's face it: Other people, circumstances, or events have a major influence on how you feel, think, and act. But to succeed, you've got to find a way to rise above all that, which means backing out of the blame game.

THE BLAME GAME

What would we do without blame? It's such a comfortable, easy path to take around stuff we'd rather avoid. It takes the pressure off in all sorts of ways—by helping us focus on all the reasons losing weight is "out of our hands." It's an easy out. For a while.

Two Ways to Play!

There are two ways to play the blame game.

Blaming the Outside

Other people:

- An unsupportive family
- Unsupportive friends

Situations or circumstances:

- Bad genes
- No time for eating healthy
- A houseful of fatty foods and no input into the grocery list
- Nothing healthy to eat at school

Bad Genes

Blaming bad genes is one of the all-time classic maneuvers. *How can you help it if you were born with a slow metabolism?*

Well, it's true, you can't change your DNA. But you *can* use what you know about your genes to overcome your weight by charting a smarter course.

Blaming the Inside

- I'm a weak person
- I don't have any willpower
- I'm just not good at planning
- I'm bad at seeing things through

Self-Blame Sucks

When you look at your diet failures, do you see a life sentence instead of a chance to learn? Do you answer the question "Why am I overweight?" with answers like "I'm weak and I have no discipline, no self-control, no willpower. It's all my fault. I wish I'd never been born. I can't do it, so why try?" Don't write yourself off before you begin! Keep reading.

Q: Okay, so I'm supposed to take responsibility for my weight—but I'm not supposed to blame myself or say it's all my fault that I'm overweight. What's the difference?

A: That's a good question, and there's a good answer. Here's the equation.

Taking responsibility	=	Being good to yourself by recognizing you owe yourself the effort and the chance to lose weight.
	BUT	
Self-blame	=	Beating yourself up.

See the difference?

Accepting responsibility means giving yourself the power to move forward and giving yourself a chance to find out how to correct the problem. Self-blame means taking that chance away from yourself. And believe me, it's just as destructive to blame yourself for your failures as it is to blame somebody or something else.

HOW TO LOSE THE BLAME— AND WIN THE PRIZE

If you're going to lose weight, do it soon, and keep it off—as I know you can—you've got to stop playing the blame game. Here are the strategies to do it.

Change the Way You Say It

I know it may sound unbelievable, but the way you talk shapes the way you view things. Take a day to listen to what you're saying when you're thinking or talking about yourself, your eating habits, your weight loss. How do you explain—to yourself or others—what's keeping you from your dream weight?

Then come back and write it down.

_____

_____

_____

_____

_____

_____

_____

_____

_____

_____

_____

_____

_____

Do any of the previous statements make you the **object or victim** of other people's actions? As in, "If Shannon hadn't insisted on going to T.G.I. Friday's, I wouldn't have been tempted to eat all that pasta" or "God, my parents really stuck me with bad genes and that's why I'm still overweight."

Do any of them make you the victim of your *own* actions or personality? As in, "My total lack of willpower keeps me from losing weight" or "If I wasn't always caving in, I wouldn't be overweight right now." These are all part of playing the blame game.

Take power by turning these statements around so that you aren't the victim but the one in control. You can do that by beginning your sentences with the word *I* and making sure that you're the one taking responsibility for what happens in your life. For instance, "I usually overeat when I'm in this situation" or "I dig out the Girl Scout cookies when the going gets rough."

Think what a difference it makes when you change "My parents stuck me with bad genes" to "I have bad genes that I need to overcome." Or changing "If my boyfriend/girlfriend wasn't always getting me to eat junk, I'd be losing weight" to "I overeat when my boyfriend/girlfriend offers me junk, and I need to find a way to break that habit."

Statements like "I stink at losing weight" and "I can't do it" don't cut it. State a fact about your behavior, not a criticism that makes you helpless. To do that, make sure your action verb is something you *did* or *are doing*, not something you *are* or *were* or *couldn't*.

Blame Game Worksheet

Now give this worksheet a try—it's important!

Write down five situations, events, or circumstances that did not go according to your diet plan—*whether or not you think they were your fault.*

Example: "My life is so busy, it makes it hard to diet."
"My sister is always picking fights with me, which forces me to get stressed and overeat junk food."

1._____

_____

_____

2._____

_____

_____

3._____

_____

_____

4._____

_____

_____

5._____

_____

_____

Now go back and read through each one. When you get to the part about what went wrong, rephrase it so that *you're* the one who's *responsible.* Remember—that's different from blame. Don't place any blame on another person, luck, or yourself.

Example: *"I don't make my diet a priority when I feel overwhelmed and busy."*
*"When I get angry at my sister, I get stressed out and
do myself harm by bingeing on junk food."*

See how these revised sentences let you take responsibility
and give you the power to make a change?

1._____

_____

_____

2._____

_____

_____

3._____

_____

_____

4._____

_____

_____

5._____

_____

_____

Excuses and Why They Stink!

A doctor has a stethoscope, a gardener has a lawn mower, a
plumber has a plunger, and a blamer has excuses. Excuses
are the tools the blamer uses to give up responsibility for
things not going the way they want.

AVOID THE IF/THEN SYNDROME

- *"If I didn't have so much work this quarter, then I'd focus more on this plan stuff."*
- *"If they just had less fatty food in the cafeteria, then I'd really be able to diet."*
- *"If my mom didn't always order pizza for dinner, then I'd eat healthier."*

If you're sitting back and waiting for the right moment for your diet to hit, don't hold your breath! Trust me, there will always be another great "if/then" sentence like the ones above to get in the way of your diet dreams. I'm not saying you don't have some valid excuses for postponing your diet, but hey, those excuses are postponing your new body, too! No matter what's going on in your life, there are *always* things you can do to get moving in the right direction.

The Top Excuses for Diet Failure

Check off the ones that apply to you:

❏ I'm big-boned.

❏ I have a slow metabolism.

❏ I can't afford to join a workout class or buy a video.

❏ Schoolwork keeps me too busy to work out.

❏ My social life is too hectic for me to focus on a diet.

❏ I'm too tired to think about what I can and can't eat.

❏ It's too late for me—it looks like I'm just destined to be overweight.

❏ I have a part-time job in a restaurant/bakery/ice cream place and the stuff's all around me, either free or discounted.

❏ I don't know where to start.

❏ It's just too hard.

❏ I'm afraid I'll hurt my bad knee if I start walking more.

❑ I'm too self-conscious about the way I look to be more active.

❑ Every time I mention wanting to get more physical, my family and friends discourage me.

❑ I have too many chores/responsibilities at home to get physical.

❑ No one I know works out.

❑ I just can't get motivated—it doesn't excite me.

❑ People should like me the way I am. *I* don't judge people by how skinny they are.

Why Excuses Make You Feel Better

Some excuses appear so airtight, they're hard to resist. They work because:

• They keep you from feeling like you've made mistakes (and if you're the one to blame, hey, you couldn't help it, you're just "made" that way).

• They protect you from blows to your self-respect (in the short run, at least).

• They help you keep a sense of control. (Hey, if it was never your responsibility, you never lost control of the situation in the first place!)

But wait a second....

Excuses Are Not Reasons

Like I said earlier, excuses are just attempts to give away responsibility. **Reasons are something very different.** They are major clues to what's made you unsuccessful in the past—what you did or didn't do that threw you off track.

Excuses are dead ends; *reasons are something you can learn from* (remember being a diet detective?).

I'm going to show you how to dig up reasons rather than excuses. The way to do it is by using Excuse Busters.

Excuse Busters!

Excuse Buster
A persuasive self-talk argument you can use to battle your excuses and take control.

THE WAR AGAINST WEIGHT

Think of this as a battle. Excuses are the enemy. What's at stake is losing weight and keeping it off. You've got to be relentless when you go into combat against the enemy—after all, it's standing in the way of victory. You need a plan of attack.

Plan of Attack

1. **Get to Know Your Enemy:** What are the excuses that keep you from losing weight?
2. **Fire Back:** Have your ammunition ready! Develop Excuse Busters that help shoot down even your strongest excuses.
3. **Outsmart Your Enemy:** Even if your Excuse Busters don't work, you're still unstoppable with a Plan B!

Get to Know Your Enemy

Which of your weight-loss promises have been the most difficult for you to stick to? Is it staying away from fatty snacks, getting more physical, cutting down on sweets and desserts, chowing down on holidays?

Write down five diet promises you tend to back out of.

Example:

1. *I'm not going to snack so much on junk.*
2. *I'm going to start swimming at the pool down the street twice a week.*
3. *I'm not going to overeat at parties and on holidays.*
4. *I'm going to pack a great, low-fat lunch for school.*
5. *I'm going to order low-cal when we eat at fast-food places.*

Now it's your turn:

1._____

_____

2._____

_____

3._____

_____

4._____

_____

5._____

_____

Now take the time to brainstorm all the excuses you use to get out of sticking to these five promises. Be honest—make sure to include all your self-doubts, fears, and insecurities: We already covered why those count! Be creative! Challenge yourself! Knowing your excuses will give you the power to fight them. Then, you **fire back with Excuse Busters.**

Fire Back!

To banish your excuses forever, you need to show no mercy. You need to have your attack planned out beforehand. Think about the excuses you just brainstormed. How can you annihilate each one, once and for all? The key is to have a powerful ready-made Excuse Buster. Here's an example of excuses and Excuse Busters:

Excuse 1: *Every time I snack on junk I think, "This one little time doesn't hurt."*

Excuse Buster: Life is made up of lots of "one little time"s. I've got to get real! *I've chosen to* lose weight and I'm going to stick to my plan. My health and self-confidence aren't worth the extra calories in "this one little time."

Excuse 2: *I'm too busy to get to the pool, I don't feel like it, I'm not capable of keeping my promises, so why bother?*

Excuse Buster: If I make getting physical a priority, I'll *find* the time to go to the pool. (I usually play Xbox for an hour after school; that's plenty of time right there.) But if the pool turns out to be too inconvenient, I'll have a plan on hand to get physical in another, more convenient way, like walking in my neighborhood. "Not feeling like it" isn't going to get me anywhere, so I'll find an activity I do feel like doing. And just because I've failed to keep my promises before doesn't mean I'm not completely capable of keeping them now—I'm not going to let myself off the hook. I won't give in or give up.

Excuse 3: *It's a special occasion. Why let all these treats pass me by since I only live once? I'm never really going to lose weight, anyway, so why waste this opportunity?*

Excuse Buster: I may only live once, but if I'm not happy during that life, and if I have to spend my time dealing with all the hassles and heartbreak of being overweight, I'm not taking very good care of myself. If I only live once, I'm going to do my best to make it great. Anyway, I'd rather pass up the opportunity to eat cookies and *take the more important opportunity* to lose this weight. Being fit will be much more satisfying than those cookies.

Excuse 4: *I'm too busy to pack my lunch. I don't know what to pack. It's boring to have a packed lunch.*

Excuse Buster: If I make eating better a priority, I'll make the time to pack my lunch. And even if I can't think of what to pack off the top of my head, there are tons of options in this book—not to mention tons more I can come up with by using the Calorie Bargains I've researched and discovered. It doesn't have to be boring, either. I will find options that are low-cal but tasty and fun.

Excuse 5: *All my friends can eat fries and cheeseburgers. Why can't I? I don't know what the lower-cal options are, anyway.*

Excuse Buster: I may have bad genes, but just deciding it's not fair isn't going to help me lose weight. I'll remember that no matter how much my friends can eat without gaining weight, it doesn't change things for me. I can find a list of low-cal fast-food options in this book (or online) and keep a copy in my wallet to remind me if I forget.

Forgetting Your Excuse Busters Is Not a Valid Excuse!

Keep this page handy. If you feel comfortable, rip it out and hang it up somewhere in your room, or keep it folded in a pocket of your backpack.

Okay, your turn. Give it some major thought and list five excuses, along with Excuse Busters for each of the excuses you listed.

1._____

_____

2._____

_____

3._____

_____

4._____

_____

5._____

_____

DIET BONUS **Make an Excuse-Buster "Piggy Bank"**

When it comes to sticking to your *Lighten Up* plan, having powerful Excuse Busters handy is like having money in the bank. So why not "bank" them? Copy each of the Excuse Busters you've come up with and put them in separate jars or bowls—one for each excuse. Then, when you "hear" yourself making that excuse, you can pull one out.

Outsmart Your Enemy: the Dreaded Unbustable Excuse

Okay, I admit it, Excuse Busting isn't foolproof. If, for example, you're injured and you can't swim, you really can't talk your way out of the problem. But those are exactly the times when you need a Plan B—or even a Plan C. If you can't swim, maybe you can walk. And if you can't walk, maybe you could do some upper-body strength training at home. Developing these alternative Excuse Busters in advance means you are *choosing* to lose weight no matter what gets in your way.

Having a Plan B means that you won't leave too many circumstances (like the weather) to chance—and let minor changes in circumstance get in the way of your weight loss. Make your own choices, not excuses, and don't let chance make choices for you.

The point is, when you take the time to think and strategize, even in the face of obstacle after obstacle, you'll be capable of getting around *any* excuse that stands in the way of your fitness.

Take a look at the examples below, then develop your own list of "unbustable" excuses and build up a store of your own Plan Bs.

Unbustable Excuse: *I have to study for exams and I don't even have time to shower, much less go for my usual walk.*

Plan B: I will bring my notes onto the StairMaster or stationary bike at the local rec center.

Plan C: Or I will do a quick, 15 or 20-minute workout tape when I need a study break, anyway. Even if I only get to work out for a few minutes, that's still better than nothing.

Unbustable Excuse: *I snack on junk when I'm stressed out over schoolwork. I really need the comfort of something to crunch on.*

Plan B: I've asked my parents to keep junk food tucked away so it doesn't tempt me.

Plan C: If the junk's still calling my name, I'll keep a bag of healthier (but still satisfying) snacks on the table and munch on those. If I can satisfy my urge to snack without going overboard on the calories, I'll be all right.

Now it's your turn to look at each one of your excuses and Excuse Busters, then try to think of any obstacles or setbacks

that might make your excuse *unbustable* and come up with a
Plan B and Plan C.

Excuse: _____

_____

Excuse Buster: _____

_____

Setback:_____

_____

Plan B:_____ `

_____

Plan C: _____

_____

Excuse: _____

_____

Excuse Buster: _____

_____

Setback:_____

_____

Plan B: _____ `

_____

Plan C: _____

_____

Excuse: _____

_____

Excuse Buster: _____

_____

Setback: _____

_____

Plan B: _____

_____

Plan C: _____

_____

Excuse: _____

_____

Excuse Buster: _____

_____

Setback: _____

_____

Plan B: _____

_____

Plan C: _____

_____

Excuse: _____

_____

Excuse Buster: _____

_____

Setback:_____

_____

Plan B: _____

_____

Plan C: _____

_____

WHAT YOU JUST GOT

You've made the brave choice to lose that weight and keep it off—and you know that the only one responsible is you. But no one is perfect, and you're sure to have moments where you want to put the responsibility on somebody else, or on circumstances beyond your control (I do, too, trust me!).

Now that you've completed this step, though, you'll have secret weapons to help you blast your way through excuses and blame.

NEXT UP

You're closing in on the end of this book at top speed! And the next step? It's all about imagination.

STEP 8 Think ... and Make It Happen

THINK YOURSELF FIT

You've got one last piece of the puzzle to go ... one last major factor in making your automatic diet work. It may sound a little strange. But I promise you, it's as necessary as any other step we've covered.

It's called visualization.

YOUR MENTAL TOOLBOX

It's true: You can use brainpower to build yourself a better body. Here's how.

Visualization: This is when you literally use your imagination to help you lose weight. The idea is to create an imagined, meaningful, detailed vision of your life *after* you've triumphed with your diet—like a movie of the future.

Mental Rehearsal: This is a *particular kind* of visualization that lets you practice, *in your mind,* how you'll behave in situations that could stand in the way of your diet. If visualization gives you a mental movie of the future, mental rehearsal lets you prepare for the scenes that could steer you into a different picture altogether (one that's not nearly as good).

WHY IT WORKS

It's not magic. If you think about it, it makes total sense.

- **It inspires you:** When you can see exactly what you're working toward, you're more likely to *act* the way you need to in order to get there.

- **It keeps you going:** Visualizing the result of all those positive food choices will keep you going when you're faced with a choice that could go either way...like whether or not to wolf down that piece of cheesecake.

- **It helps you nail down the details:** If you were creating an actual movie set, how would you know where to put every prop if you didn't have a clear vision of the finished product? Daydreaming helps you figure out the details that'll help you reach your big result.

- **It helps you plan for obstacles:** Visualization and mental rehearsal give you the chance to anticipate the "rough" times (such as Diet Busters, Eating Alarm Times, and unconscious eating, to name a few!) and plan how to blast right through them.

DAYDREAMING WITH A PURPOSE

I know it may *still* sound weird. I've had plenty of clients laugh at the idea of *imagining* a thinner future in order to make it happen. But it's funny how quickly they stop laughing when they see that it works.

Megan Quann, the sixteen-year-old swimmer who beat the defending Olympic champion, Penny Heyns of South Africa, in the 100-meter breaststroke in Sydney, used visualization to lead her to victory. Quann had promised at the American Olympic trials that Heyns was "going down," and every night before the event, she took a stopwatch to bed and visualized her race stroke by stroke. "I can see the tiles at the bottom of the pool, I can hear the crowd cheering, I can taste the water," Quann said of her ritual.

YOUR GREAT WEIGHT DESTINATION!

In order to diet right, you need to know what it'll feel like to get where you're going. It's kind of like sending a *postcard to yourself* as a reminder: ***This* is why it's worth it.**

LIFE PRESERVERS

One of the best ways to use visualization and mental rehearsal is to create something I call a "Life Preserver."

A **Life Preserver** is a *positive,* visualized, and fully imagined future event or situation that is tough enough to stand up to your worst food crisis. It helps you remember why you wanted to lose weight in the first place and remain focused on your goal.

With your Life Preservers in hand, you'll have the power to walk away from the fudge, the fries, or the fettuccine. And since we're going to plan them right now, you'll be ready to do it automatically, at those make-or-break moments that come along when you least expect them.

Create Your Life Preservers

Try to visualize three events or situations that could occur once you reach your weight-loss goal. The purpose here is to have three *positive* scenarios you can keep in your back pocket, backpack, or wallet to pull out when you're having a tough time sticking to your plan. Make them as inspiring as you possibly can—after all, they need to be able to *keep you afloat* even during your toughest food dilemmas.

TIPS

1. **Make them *detailed:*** You should be able to smell, see, and hear this future moment. What will you look like when you lose the weight? How will you feel? How will your life be different?

2. **Make them *inspiring:*** The more inspiring they are, the more they'll really mean to you when you're in need.

3. **List *events:*** Use upcoming events as a way to set the stage for your visualization. For example, imagine going to the prom after losing twenty pounds, or going on vacation with your family and looking great on the beach.

4. **Write them down and keep them *available:*** Make sure your visualizations are at your fingertips at all times. Maybe even copy them onto a back page of your planner, or onto an index card you keep in your purse or wallet.

5. ***Relax:*** Don't worry if you can't visualize a slimmer, healthier you right away; experts say that it can take some time. Instead, start with the future event itself, and over time the rest of the details will work themselves out.

Here are a few examples to help you get started.

Example: *"I walk into school on the first day of the year and I've lost 25 pounds. At the lockers, I see some friends I haven't seen all summer. They pass me by at first because they don't even recognize me, and then I say "hi" and they look at me in shock. They can't believe it! They say I look great and I know they really mean it. All day, it's more of the same: people who know me look at me like they're seeing a whole new side of me. I feel confident, happy, and proud."*

Example: *"My dad is always 'joking' that my sister got her looks from my mom, and I got the 'big-bone' genes from him. When I started my diet he did this annoying thing where he was like, 'Good for you,' but then acted the opposite way, constantly shoving pancakes in front of me at breakfast and telling me, 'One little slice of pie won't hurt,' after dinner. He obviously doesn't believe in my diet, or in me and my ability to lose the weight.*

"Well, here's my Life Preserver: It's six months from now and I come into the house from a nice jog around the block, looking thin and healthy in these cool sweats I just bought last week. He's in the kitchen eating that pie, and I sit down at the table, grab an apple, and eat that, the picture of a thin, fit girl. The jokes about being big-boned have stopped—and these days, it's a toss-up as to who got the looks in the family."

Ask Yourself These Questions for a Jump Start

- **What will I look like when I lose weight permanently?**
- **How will I feel?** You've accomplished stuff before. If you're having trouble, try transferring those feelings to this situation.
- **How will my life be different?** Think specifics—how will going to stores, to school, to parties be different?
- **How will others in my life react to me?** Don't be afraid to name names!
- **What will it be like to feel better *physically*?** Try to imagine what it would be like to have more energy and less weight to carry around.

Your Turn

Now you try it. Sit somewhere comfortable, allow yourself to dream about the future you, then write down all your thoughts—every last one of them. Use your notebook if you need more space. Get three major scenarios down on paper and continue to add to them, including more and more details and feelings. Incorporate *all* your senses until your Life Preserver takes on the quality of a real experience.

_____

_____

_____

_____

_____

_____

_____

_____

_____

_____

Revenge Is Sweet

Have you ever heard the expression "Living well is the best revenge?" Come on—dish the dirt! We all have someone from the past we want to look great for and then walk away from. Nobody said your Life Preserver had to be worthy of a Nobel Peace Prize! So, who is it that you'd like to run into in your Life Preserver visualization? An ex-boyfriend or -girlfriend? A competitive friend? A person who betrayed you? A cynical PE teacher? If it's *inspiring,* go for it.

Picture Your Reward

Do you have any pictures of yourself at a weight you loved? If you've never been at a great weight, look through magazines (like *Shape, Fitness, Self*) to find a picture of someone who has features similar to yours, and who is roughly the weight you want to be. Paper-clip or staple the picture into these pages and use it as a tool for developing a clear vision of your future self. (Oh, and leave people like the Rock or paper-thin models from *Cosmo* out of the picture. You *should* dream big—but these ideals are not realistic and, a lot of times, not even healthy.)

Are you done? Is each Life Preserver a clear, detailed, *real* experience in your mind? Here are some more tips to make them that way.

Pull Out Concrete Reminders

Do you have a bathing suit you'd like to fit into? A ticket for an event you'd love to look great for? Do you have keepsakes that remind you of times you've succeeded (like trophies, blue ribbons, photos)? Pull out these physical reminders and let them be brain food for your daydreams. Summon up the feelings of fitting into that suit, or what it felt like to win that award. Use this stuff as inspiration.

YOU'VE GOT A STARRING ROLE—REHEARSE!

Mental rehearsal is going to make you the star, screenwriter, and director of your life by helping you know *in advance* how you're going to react to disastrous diet moments.

Everyone uses some type of mental rehearsal throughout the day. When you imagine how you're going to pull an A in English, or what you're going to do over the weekend, or what you're going to say to convince your parents to let you have a cell phone, these are, in a way, forms of mental rehearsal.

Mental rehearsal actually gives your brain a chance to practice your life choices.

In a way, it's like learning to ride a bike. With dieting you need to develop new ways of balancing in order not to fall off, so you keep on practicing until it comes naturally.

Luckily, you don't have to *actually* practice standing in the buffet line at your cousin's wedding to "learn" how to turn down fattening food. Instead, you can rehearse the scenario in your mind. The point is, mental rehearsal gets your brain practiced and ready to make healthy choices on those occasions when you're tempted to do the opposite. When you imagine the script in advance, you'll be ready to act your part to perfection. And you'll get a glimpse of how good you'll look doing it. What better reason could you have to make it automatic?

> Can you rehearse for every single diet obstacle? I doubt it. But the more you plan and think about those "rough" times, the more you'll be in control.

Mental Rehearsal Worksheet

Time to dive in.

1. **Find an obstacle:** Go back and flip through pages 101–130 and pick a challenge: an unconscious or mindless eating pattern, an Eating Alarm Time, or a Diet Buster.

Your challenge:

_____

Now think about how you'd *roughly* like to change your behavior when you meet that challenge—include the thoughts and emotions you want to have and the actions you want to take in your "ideal" version. Jot them down.

How I *want* to deal (ideal scenario):

_____

_____

_____

_____

_____

2. **Add details:** Now start to add the nitty-gritty details. Break it all down into little steps—picture how you would act and behave to protect your healthy and perfectly satisfying eating habits, and write it down. Don't spare a thought, no matter how tiny or insignificant it might seem.

The details:

_____

_____

_____

_____

_____

_____

_____

3. **Tell the whole story:** Now you're ready to write a step-by-step description of exactly what your ideal experience would be like _from beginning to end._ Be creative and thoughtful here. _Visualize_ what it will take for you to get through this situation.

The scenario from beginning to end:

_____

_____

_____

_____

_____

_____

_____

_____

4. **Make it come alive:** Once you have the general script down, go back to make the experience really come alive. Use all your senses. Embellish until you feel like you're there.

The scenario in living color:

_____

_____

_____

_____

_____

_____

_____

_____

_____

5. **Revisit your mental rehearsal situation often:** Give it power by telling yourself it's real and reachable.

6. **Rerun the scenario in your head whenever you find yourself about to live out the situation you've rehearsed:** The details should be as familiar to you as the words and notes to your favorite song.

Repeat as Needed

Once you've developed a scenario you feel good about, stop to congratulate yourself... and then try another one in your notebook. Or, if you don't feel like writing your rehearsals, use the guidelines above to do them in your head. You can't have too many!

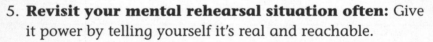

If you fail to plan, you plan to fail. Rehearse and you'll get the gold!

JUST SAY NO!

Do you *really* know how to say no? Being able to do it for real is one of the most important skills you can have.

Even the most well-meaning people are bound to ask you to do things that aren't right for you. Let's say, for example, you're at the movies and your friend asks you to share a large popcorn. You have to ask yourself if popcorn's what you *really* want, and if it isn't, you have to be ready to say no.

Write down three occasions when your friends, family, or loved ones have put you in a situation that made you uncomfortable saying no to food.

Example: *I was at a big family dinner and everyone was eating huge plates of food. Aunt Tracy kept nagging me to eat more, and when I'd say, "No, thanks," she'd say things like "Oh, come on, don't you like my cheesecake?" When it comes to food, Aunt Tracy just won't take no for an answer.*

Now it's your turn:

1. _____

_____

2. _____

_____

_____

3. _____

_____

_____

Now brainstorm responses to these types of situations so you'll be armed with an automatic answer the next time one rolls around.

Example:

Situation 1: *My aunt wants me to eat everything in sight, even when I tell her I'm not hungry.*

What I say: *I DO love your cooking, but I'm really full and I couldn't eat another bite. No cheesecake for me!*

Now it's your turn (use your notebook if you need more space).

Situation 1: _____

_____

What you say: _____

_____

What you're thinking: _____

_____

Situation 2: _____

_____

What you say: _____

_____

What you're thinking: _____

_____

Situation 3: _____

_____

What you say: _____

_____

What you're thinking: _____

_____

TALK—AND BELIEVE IT!

You may be constantly telling yourself, "I can't lose weight—it's just too difficult," or "I'll never be able to get out there and work out every day," or "I can't eat at Ruby Tuesday's without ordering a burger with fries." But hey, you're the one in charge of your life; do you really want to be the one convincing yourself you won't succeed?

An **affirmation** is a strong positive statement that assumes that something you want to be true is actually true. It's another way of "talking to yourself about yourself," in a good way.

If you're constantly putting yourself down, try to:

* Make yourself aware of your own thoughts.
* Replace negative thoughts with positive ones.
* Reinforce those positive thoughts and feelings with affirmations.

You probably remember the book *The Little Engine That Could*. In it, a choo-choo train overcomes its challenges by chanting over and over, "I think I can, I think I can."

But affirmations aren't just for kids! When you practice and repeat them, they really *can* give you the power to chug ahead.

Overcome the Corniness Factor

You may laugh at yourself when you start to use affirmations, and that's fine. Affirmations do sound funny at first. But eventually they will actually help you think of yourself as someone who can achieve your dreams.

Not Up for It?

At the very least, make sure to put a stop to all the *negative* self-talk, where you tell yourself you can't do something.

If you have trouble with schoolwork, an affirmation might go: "I am capable of getting good grades." For your weight, the affirmation might be: "I deserve to look the way I *want* to look." Gradually, the mind will respond and you will begin to experience results.

Go ahead, write down a few affirmations for weight loss— and anything else that comes to mind. Put them in the present tense ("I am capable of working out every day"), and repeat them to yourself either as a kind of meditation or whenever you face a situation that threatens to stress you out or damage your self-esteem.

My Affirmations

_____

_____

_____

_____

_____

_____

_____

_____

_____

_____

_____

_____

_____

WHAT YOU JUST GOT

Visualization, mental rehearsal, and self-talk: They're all ways to use your imagination to create real, physical results. And when you're making important changes in your life, you can use all the help you can get.

Just keep at it for a little while. It'll get easier and easier and more and more automatic. And you'll see it affect way more than your head.

NEXT UP

You're almost there! The next-to-last step! Turn the page and get ready to pull it all together....

STEP 9 Make a Road Map

ARE WE THERE YET?

You wouldn't take a road trip without mapping out your route, so why start a diet without having a plan? With any trip, you need to think ahead, know what your next move is going to be, and then your next move after that. For your diet to be a success, you need a plan.

A ROAD MAP TO THE FITTER YOU

I know, I know—planning probably sounds boring, maybe even a little hard. Isn't just *deciding* to make better choices enough?

Well, remember the 98% of people whose diets fail? Too many of those people started out *deciding* to lose weight, too. The problem is, they didn't have a plan for how to make it happen.

Weird as it sounds, planning your diet means you actually get to be spontaneous—because you've already decided how to handle all your food choices in advance. And by now you should have the answers and tactics from all the stuff you've read in the past steps—now it's time to put it all together.

This Way to a Fitter You

Basically, this step is going to help you put together a fool-proof diet plan. Consider it a road map to your great weight destination. It'll show you how to:

- Lay out your route.
- Prepare for obstacles and detours.
- Find interesting and exciting ways to make the trip go faster.
- Avoid the most tempting roadside attractions.
- Make it second nature...and put it on cruise control.

Once you've made your plan, you won't have to diet harder to get the body you want...because you'll be dieting *smarter*.

Power to the Planners

According to the *Journal of the American Dietetic Association,* people who set specific plans for their diets have an 84% better chance of losing and keeping off weight than those who don't.

GETTING SMARTER

People do crazy things to lose weight. We've already talked about some of them: drinking only milk shakes, cutting out every vegetable with a carb count above 10. But the people who really succeed at losing weight do it without trendy diets, by making changes that *make sense.*

There's an easy way for you to do the same thing. It involves getting to know yourself a little better—and it can be summed up in the word **smarter**.

Be Specific: Know exactly what you want.

Get Motivated: Come up with ways to keep yourself inspired.

Make It Achievable: Set your sights on something challenging but possible.

Know Your Rewards: It may seem obvious, but...what are you losing weight for, anyway?

Get Tactical: You've got skills, so use them!

Evaluate Yourself: How will you know you're winning if you don't keep score?

Be Ready to Revise: Things change. Get ready to adapt.

Be Specific

Knowing you want to lose weight is a good start, but to make it happen, you need to think about the *how, when, where,* and *why* of losing that weight.

Think about what you want from your diet. Make it clear and specific, like "I want to lose 15 pounds by December 1st." The key is to set your sights on the weight you want and then start planning—very specifically—how to get there. That'll make it feel real—and that's crucial.

For now, you can start by answering these simple questions. There is no right or wrong answer, so don't be afraid to think big (or skinny).

• How much weight do I want to lose, total?

_____

• How soon do I want to lose it?

_____

Now let's take your goal and turn it into something even more specific.

Here's an example:

You say, "I want to lose 15 pounds in six months." Now think about *how* you can do that.

1. To lose 15 pounds in six months, you would have to cut 52,500 calories from your current diet or burn that many extra calories. (Remember, to lose one pound of fat, you have to burn 3,500 calories more than you eat.)

2. That breaks down to about 290 calories per day.

3. It's easy to set a specific goal from there: You could come up with a way to cut 150 calories from your diet and burn 150 calories through exercise. As you'll see in the steps that follow, that's easy enough—and by making it specific, you'll know exactly what you need to do.

Now it's your turn:

1. To lose_____pounds in_____months, you need to cut and/or burn_____calories. (Remember—it's 3,500 calories per pound of fat, so to get the number of calories, multiply 3,500 by the number of pounds.)

2. That means you need to cut and/or burn_____calories per day. (Divide the number of days by the number of calories.)

3. Now you're ready to set goals for how to cut those calories each day.

Don't Want to Do the Math?

To make it even easier, you can use an online weight-loss calculator to get this info. Try: caloriesperhour.com and go to Weight Loss Calculator.

How Do I Know What's Reasonable?
Shoot to loose no more than 4 to 6 pounds in a month—that's enough. Also, check with a medical doctor.

Goal Setting Got You Spooked?
Having a goal is the same as admitting that you want something, and wanting something can make you feel pretty vulnerable. Why? Because it opens you up to the possibility of *not* getting what you want. **Don't let this stop you!** Setting a specific goal—right here and now—only proves you're serious about taking charge of your weight—and that means giving yourself the power to make it happen.

Get *M*otivated

Has this ever happened to you? You decide to diet, to exercise three times a week, to eat 1,200 calories a day. And then you just get tired of it. You lose your enthusiasm. Good-bye, diet, good-bye, better body. You need motivators.

A motivator is something that excites you and helps to keep you on track. It gives you a reason to *enjoy* sticking to your diet and the *energy* to keep moving down the road. Nobody wants to stay with a routine that's boring—and who can blame them? Eventually, a boring routine will cause you to lose momentum and stray off course. Don't leave it up to your willpower keep you on track—the key to making your new routine stick is making it fun...with motivators.

Let's say you've decided to exercise. Which of these sounds like a better plan?

a. "I'm going to go for a run every morning before school!"

b. "I'm going to take the long way to class every day. I have five minutes between each class, so I might as well use them."

You might think the first choice sounds better, but it depends. It might not work for you if when the alarm goes off and it's still dark outside, the last thing you really want to do is crawl out from under the covers and start running.

Don't enjoy exercise? Think about the ideas we talked about in Step 6. For example, what about things that don't really feel like exercise, like maybe biking, swimming, tennis, or volleyball? Still too much? What about just walking to the convenience store instead of asking your mom for a ride? Walking may not burn calories as fast as running, but it *will burn* calories—and any additional calories you burn will help you lose weight.

See, the key to staying motivated is to work activities and eating habits into your life—in a way you are going to stick with. It should be fun...and automatic. To make it that way, you've got to plan it.

Which would you rather do? (Circle one)

Go for a 20-minute jog *or* bike around with your friends for an hour?

Walk on a treadmill at the local community center for 40 minutes *or* walk around the mall for 40 minutes?

Drink a weight-loss shake *or* make your own low-fat smoothie?

Can you make any of these options part of a routine? Is it something that can keep you motivated for the long haul? If yes, great. If not, stay tuned—review the past steps, and swap the old ideas for new ones, until you find the ones that work.

Make It *Achievable*

While your strategy needs to be something that gets you excited, it also needs to be realistic. Making a promise you can't keep could leave you discouraged and frustrated, and that's dangerous to your diet, because it could make you want to abandon it altogether.

Don't worry. There's a way to safeguard your plan against this kind of frustration. To find out whether your goal is actually doable, just ask yourself these three simple questions.

1. *Am I giving myself enough time?*

Believe me, I know you want to be in shape as soon as you can. But while it's definitely possible to start losing weight immediately, you'll want to steer clear of putting a crazy time frame on your diet. Why?

Because rushing your diet—and making sky-high promises— will set you up for a major crash. And don't forget about that research I mentioned—the faster you lose weight, the faster you gain it back.

So...

Instead of saying, "I'm going to lose 20 pounds in two weeks," try, "I'm going to lose 10 pounds over the next three months by making my diet automatic and using all the strategies I read in this book. I'm in no rush, because I know that the weight will never come back."

2. *Is it possible but challenging?*

On top of doing crazy things to lose weight, people also make amazing promises when they're just starting their diets. "I'm going to run at six A.M. every day!" "I'm giving up fries for good!"

If you love running and getting up early, or if you hate fries, I guess this is doable. But generally, these extreme statements aren't true in the long run, and you'll probably cave eventually. That's because—drumroll, please—you're human!

Unless you have a will of steel and a red cape to match, you probably won't stick to a plan that's crazy ambitious.

The reality is: **Setting your sights too high is the surest way to diet disaster!**

Nobody can stick to a plan that's too difficult, at least not for very long; it's a surefire setup for failure. And this kind of failure is a drag for more than just the obvious reasons: On top of keeping you from your goal, it blasts your confidence. And you want to *build* your confidence, not destroy it, right?

On the other hand, the *second*-surest way to diet disaster is to set your sights too low. Promising to go for a walk around the block once a week and getting to it only if and when you have the time isn't going to get you any further than wild promises to run a marathon by next month. And when you set your sights too low, you'll soon start wondering what the point is, because you won't be getting any results.

Never Say Never

Watch out for promises like "I'll never have a piece of chocolate cake (or an order of fries) again." Using words like *always*, *must*, *ever*, or *never* puts a lot of pressure on you to be perfect, and nobody is. Not to mention that once a food is forbidden, you'll probably want it even more.

For your plan to be achievable, it's got to be *possible* but *challenging*. You've got to find a combination that's just right.

Here are some examples of **achievable** vs. **unachievable** goals.

Too High (Unachievable): "I'll lose 20 pounds a week."

Too Low (Unachievable): "I'll lose 3 pounds when I get to it."

Just Right (Achievable): "I'll lose at least 1 pound a week until I get to my ideal weight. And if I don't, I will work on improving my plan."

3. *Can I control it?*

Is the goal you're setting something you yourself can control? Or are you making a promise that, truthfully, is in someone else's hands?

A goal like "I'm going to look so good once this diet is over, I'll be a professional model" might give you plenty of motivation at first—but you can't control whether or not it's going to happen.

BE REAL

Remember, getting thin and fit won't necessarily give you Carmen Electra's curves or the Rock's cut body, but that doesn't mean you can't shed all that extra weight—and have a much fitter, healthier you.

Your Turn...

Think of three specific things you can do to achieve your diet goal and write them in the blanks below. Make sure to keep them challenging but realistic.

Example: *Calorie Bargain—I'm going to substitute salad for fries at lunch four times a week.*

Example: *I'm going to go for a 10-minute run three times a week and increase that to 15 minutes after a month.*

1. _____

_____

2. _____

_____

3. _____

_____

Know Your *Rewards*

No doubt you've fantasized about the thinner, healthier you. You've probably pictured looking better, feeling better—maybe even proving your strength to someone who didn't believe in you or getting the attention of someone who's never even noticed you.

But it's not always easy to keep those pictures in view, and it can be downright difficult when that extra piece of chocolate cake is staring you in the face.

Having your Life Preservers on paper and looking at them often will help you. Thinking about this stuff helps you to make an *emotional connection* to your goals—and that can help you get through the rough times.

DIET BONUS   Keep a copy of your Life Preservers and post it beside your bed or inside a drawer you use every day. If you're comfortable (and you may not be), post it on the door of your family's fridge so that it's staring you in the face when you go to reach for that tub of ranch dip or that leftover pizza.

Get *T*actical

Losing weight should never be about luck. And winging it won't cut it. To get it done, you've got to get tactical.

A tactic is a way to make your own luck—by anticipating your obstacles and weak spots and coming up with ways to deal. This entire book has given you all the tactics you need to make your diet automatic. Here are some reminders of great tactics.

Example: *If my friends plan a group trip to McDonald's, I'll decide what I'm ordering before I get there. I can even say, "Great, I'll get one of the salads with the Paul Newman low-cal dressing— I love that." Then, when we get there, they'll all expect me to order the salad and I'll be more likely to do it.*

Example: *If my mom begs me to eat seconds at dinner, I'll tell her I'm stuffed. But I'll ask her to pack me a small container of left-overs for lunch the next day—that way she'll know I liked the meal, plus I won't have to eat the fattening cafeteria food tomorrow.*

*E*valuate Yourself

Imagine you're on a long road trip. You didn't know how far you'd gone or even if you were headed in the right direction. If that were true, you wouldn't have a clue how much farther you had to go or whether you needed to turn around and take a different route!

In the same way, it's important to have a method of measuring your diet's success so you know whether your plan is working...or whether you need to change direction.

Here are some easy ways to evaluate your diet progress.

- Weigh yourself once a week (not daily), and keep track of the results in your notebook. Remember, your weight shifts slightly from hour to hour, so don't weigh yourself obsessively or worry if a pound or two seems to appear out of nowhere.

- Do you have a pair of pants that fits you *perfectly?* If not, can you buy a pair? (They don't have to look good— they're not really for *wearing.*) Keep these pants in the back of your closet and try them on once a week. Gauge whether you're gaining or losing weight by how snugly or loosely they fit.

ASK THE RIGHT QUESTIONS

Asking questions is the most powerful way to evaluate your progress. Here are some questions you'll want to ask yourself as you move forward with your diet.

- Are these changes I'm willing to make forever?
- What would I like to do that I'm not doing and that could help my diet succeed?
- What new risks and challenges am I willing to face in order to lose weight?
- What's standing in the way of the changes I need to make to get the body I want?

Revise When You Need To

It's almost bound to happen: You'll have times when you realize you're not getting fitter as fast as you'd like—or in the way that you've planned.

Maybe you set a goal of losing 2 pounds a week, and you've only been losing one. Maybe you said you'd jog around the block four times a week, but you've decided you *hate* jogging.

Does that mean you should just throw up your hands in despair?

No way! When your plan isn't quite working for you, it's simply time to revise your tactics. Being ready to revise is a major key to your success, and you're not likely to win without it.

If you planned to lose a pound a week, and you're only losing one every two weeks—think about the small changes you can make to speed the weight loss—like upping the amount of physical activity you do and/or switching from full-fat to nonfat milk and/or substituting Ben & Jerry's low-fat frozen Cherry Garcia yogurt for Ben & Jerry's ice cream.

The compromises you choose are up to you. As long as you're willing to adapt, you'll be able to revise your plan to make it work.

Here's an easy way to figure out what's working for you: Write down each goal or tactic you came up with each week to see how easy it was for you to keep it up.

Examples:

My goal: *I want to eat a low-fat cereal every morning for breakfast.*

Is it working? *It was easy most mornings, but I overslept one day.*

My goal: *I want to play tennis every day after school.*

Is it working? *Even when I can actually get up the motivation, it's hard to convince my friends to play.*

WHAT YOU JUST GOT

Congratulations—you've set specific goals, you know how to make them achievable, and you've pinned down some motivators. You've got a firm grasp on some future rewards, and you're creating the tactics to make those rewards a reality. You also know how to evaluate and revise your tactics so that you can get there as quickly as possible.

NEXT UP

You've done all the hard work; now it's time to put everything you've learned together and get ready to lose weight *for good*.

STEP 10 A Blueprint for Your Life

You've done it. You've arrived at the final step. You've already started to think about eating, your weight, and getting physical in a whole new way. You've discovered the patterns that hold you back and figured out how to break them. Now all that's left is to pull it together. Once you do that, you can go out and make it happen.

In this step, you're going to get your basic info on paper. Why? So that from here on out, you'll have it at a glance, to come back to when you need it to keep you reminded, keep you motivated, keep you on track, and keep it automatic.

You're going to have that body you want, for good. This step is your blueprint.

SAMPLE PLAN

THE OVERALL GOAL

Lose 35 pounds forever!!!

MIDTERM GOALS

Lose 20 pounds in the next nine months and change my style of eating and physical activity.

THE STRATEGY: SPECIFIC DETAILS AND SUB-GOALS

Twenty pounds in nine months. This means I need to drop 70,000 calories—or about 250 calories per day from what I'm used to consuming. I'll make sure my Calorie Bargains add up to 200 calories per day. Then I'll up my physical activity by about 50 calories per day (like walking for an extra 10 minutes).

RESULTS OF THREE-DAY FOOD CHALLENGE:
MY MAJOR CALORIE BARGAINS

- *Bottled water instead of a medium soda at McDonald's (save 200 calories)*
- *Low-calorie vinaigrette instead of blue cheese salad dressing (save 175 calories)*
- *Fat-free chocolate pudding instead of brownies (save 97 calories)*
- *Skim milk instead of whole milk (save 60 calories)*

GETTING PHYSICAL

I need to do my physical activity on weekend mornings and get it out of the way, otherwise I won't do it. Those mornings, I will walk on the hiking trail up by the park near my house. It will be perfect. During the week, I'm going to try to weave in an additional 30 minutes per day. This will be pretty easy. I usually go to the mall at least once a week, so I'll walk around there for a set amount of time. I'm also going to start mowing the lawn once a week for my dad; I like doing outside chores, anyway. I'm going to keep workout tapes on hand and do one at least twice a week (I'll do low-impact at first!). And I'm going to start walking our dog around my neighborhood.

OBSTACLES, SLIPUPS, OR POTENTIAL SETBACKS
I MAY ENCOUNTER IN PURSUING MY GOAL

Eating Alarm Times, Unconscious Eating, or Diet Busters

a. *On holidays, I tend to overeat and throw my diet out the window.*

b. *Lunchtime at school—the unhealthiest options always seem to be the most tempting.*

c. *I go out with my friends for fast food on the weekends.*

d. *Late-night snacking: right after dinner, I'm ready to sit in front of the TV and have a bag of potato chips or ice cream. It's one or the other. And I know that brushing my teeth to avoid this craving is not going to cut it!!*

e. *If I think I already messed up my diet, I start eating everything in sight.*

WAYS TO OVERCOME THESE OBSTACLES, SLIPUPS, OR POTENTIAL SETBACKS

a. *On holidays, I'll make sure I have lots of lower-fat goodies on hand and that I'll let myself have a little, but I won't overdo it. I'll concentrate on avoiding unconscious nibbling, and when I'm really tempted to overeat, I'll visualize my ideal weight to remind me of what's at stake.*

b. *I will pack a good, tasty lunch and leave my money at home.*

c. *Before we park at McDonald's, I'll mentally rehearse going in and ordering a grilled chicken sandwich without mayo, and no fries. This will be instead of the large burger, fries, and a soda I usually have.*

d. *Again, I'm going to prepare for late-night cravings by thinking in advance. I'll know what healthy snacks are around to munch on. I put air-popped popcorn on our shopping list. It's only about 60 calories for two full cups and it tastes really good. I also don't mind munching on fruit. I will also try to make sure I have my Life Preservers handy.*

e. *I will mentally rehearse "cheating" and what happens next. It will not be an excuse to overeat. Instead I will reach for one of my Calorie Bargains and not go crazy bingeing.*

EXCUSES I MIGHT USE TO PULL ME FROM MY GOALS

a. *I really do have a slow metabolism, and it's so hard to pay attention to everything I eat.*

b. *I get embarrassed figuring out the healthier items on the menu in front of my friends. I hate calling attention to my diet—it's like calling attention to my weight.*

c. *My parents still have the same old eating habits, and the dinner table's packed with fatty foods to tempt me.*

d. *Sometimes I eat a low-fat snack, but I end up eating so much of it, I might as well be eating the fattier version.*

EXCUSE BUSTERS

a. *Yes, I may have a slow metabolism, but I realize that I can make my new eating adjustments automatic and get the weight off.*

b. *If my friends and I are meeting at the restaurant, I will call the restaurant right before I leave home and ask them about healthier options over the phone. I have less of a problem asking over the phone than in front of my friends. If we end up at the place on a whim, I'll use what I know about Calorie Bargains (leave off the mayo, order grilled instead of fried, leave off sides like french fries) to make the most diet-friendly decision I can.*

c. *I will have my own low-cal meal prepared by the time the other food's on the table. Once I'm done and my stomach's satisfied, I'll make sure that if I'm still tempted to eat the fatty stuff, I'll leave the table and spend my time doing something else.*

d. *I need to be conscious of how much I'm eating. It's not that hard to pay attention to what's going into my mouth and whether I'm overdoing it. Also, if I'm still hungry, I can snack on veggies or some other fiber-filled snack that'll fill me up without laying on the calories.*

LONG-TERM REWARDS

a. *Fit into a great-looking bathing suit*

b. *Feel healthier and more energetic*

c. *Be happier*

d. *Increase self-confidence*

LIFE PRESERVERS

a. *Running into my crush over the summer*

b. *Having people who teased me about my weight see how good I look*

c. *Feeling good about how I look when I lie on the beach over vacation*

NOW IT'S YOUR TURN

The Overall Goal

How much weight do you want to lose?

_____

Midterm Goals

What are your goals in the meantime? To get more physical and eat healthier? To have a certain number of pounds gone by Christmas or summer break? *Remember to be realistic!*

_____

_____

_____

_____

_____

_____

_____

_____

_____

_____

The Strategy: Specific Details and Sub-goals

Get specific! How are you going to get to your goal? How many calories do you need to cut per day? What are some of the ways you can do that? How many calories do you want to burn getting physical?

_____

_____

_____

_____

_____

_____

_____

_____

Results of Three-Day Food Challenge: My Major Calorie Bargains

List the Calorie Bargains you're most likely to use every day.

_____

_____

_____

_____

_____

_____

_____

_____

Physical Activity Increase

When will you increase your physical activity? What's likely and doable? (Weekday afternoons? Weekday mornings before school? What about on the weekends?) What sort of activities will you do? Where will you do them?

_____

_____

_____

_____

_____

_____

_____

_____

Obstacles, Slipups, or Potential Setbacks I May Encounter in Pursuing my Goal

What are your Eating Alarm Times, unconscious-eating moments, and Diet Busters?

_____

_____

_____

_____

_____

_____

_____

_____

_____

Ways to Overcome These Obstacles, Slipups, or Potential Setbacks

Plan in advance for your Eating Alarm Times, unconscious-eating moments, and Diet Busters.

_____

_____

_____

_____

_____

_____

_____

_____

_____

_____

_____

_____

_____

_____

_____

_____

_____

_____

_____

_____

Excuses I Might Use to Pull Me from My Goals

Make sure you include the toughest ones you've got, like bad genes or unhealthy family habits that surround you.

_____

_____

_____

_____

_____

_____

_____

_____

_____

_____

_____

_____

_____

_____

_____

_____

_____

_____

_____

_____

_____

_____

_____

_____

Excuse Busters

Find a buster (or two or three) for every one of those excuses!

_____

_____

_____

_____

_____

_____

_____

_____

_____

_____

_____

_____

_____

_____

_____

_____

_____

_____

_____

_____

_____

_____

_____

_____

Long-Term Rewards

What are the real rewards for getting to your ideal weight?
What kind of great stuff will that bring into your life?

_____

_____

_____

_____

_____

_____

_____

_____

_____

Life Preservers

Picture the payoff. What kind of triumphant future events or
situations can you picture that are so good, they'll pull you
through your toughest diet moments?

_____

_____

_____

_____

_____

_____

_____

_____

Final Word

You've just read the only book you'll ever need to help you lose weight and keep it off forever. A part of me wishes I could jump off the pages and be with you over the next year to put you on the right track, but the truth is, you have what you need right here. I know for sure that if you follow these words—even just some of them—you can lose weight permanently. No more quick-fix diets, no more worries about what you can and can't eat, no more unhappy shopping days, and no more uncomfortable situations because you're overweight. This ends now and forever.

If you really want this, you can make it happen—not tomorrow, but right here, right now.

Acknowledgments

This book has been a long time coming, and I have many people to thank for helping me finally bring it to fruition.

First, I would like to thank my literary agent, Scott Waxman, a calm force in my turbulent, busy life. He believed in me from the start and is a real friend.

Next, Jodi Anderson, for her dedication, excitement, and her unyielding commitment to help to connect the material to readers of any age.

Liesa Abrams, who has been a passionate advocate in getting this book produced, a great editor, a wonderful mediator, and a smart marketer. I also want to thank her for understanding and believing in me as an author and as a person.

I would like to thank Judy Kern for her consistent help and assistance—and attention to detail.

Also, Kara Higgins Wahlgren, for helping to set the stage for what's become a wonderful and helpful handbook for anyone who wants to eat right and stay sane.

Carole McCarthy, MSW, for helping to crystallize the behaviors necessary to help others help themselves.

Lastly, I would also like to thank Alan Barnett for a great cover (with guidance from Kristen Pettit), and Alicia Fox and Alan Barnett for those amazing interior pages, all helping bring the words and book to life.

Index